FEVER!

The biography of

JOHN TRAVOLTA

Douglas Thompson, international journalist and biographer, is a regular contributor to major publications worldwide. His books include, *Like A Virgin: Madonna Revealed*, which was an international bestseller in 1991, and the biographies of Sharon Stone, Michelle Pfeiffer, Dudley Moore and Clint Eastwood. Douglas Thompson was based in Los Angeles for 20 years and now lives with his wife and daughter in their farmhouse near Cambridge.

FEVER!
The biography of
JOHN TRAVOLTA

Douglas Thompson

B🌿XTREE

for Dandy, for being cool

First published in Great Britain in 1996 by
Boxtree Limited, Broadwall house, 21 Broadwall, London SE1 9PL.

10 9 8 7 6 5 4 3 2 1

Design: Nigel Davies at Stone Studio
Printed and bound in the United Kingdom by Bath Press

A CIP catalogue entry for this book is available from the British Library.

ISBN: 0 7522 1074 2

Picture Acknowledgements:
The publisher would like to thank the following for pictures in the plate section: London Features International Ltd for pictures on p. 1 and p. 6 (bottom) and Kevin Mazur/ London Features International Ltd for picture on p. 7 (bottom); Paramount Pictures Corp/Ronald Grant for pictures on p. 2 (top) and p. 4 (top), Universal Pictures/ Ronald Grant for picture on p. 3 (bottom), Miramax/Ronald Grant for picture on p. 7 (top), Touchstone Pictures/Ronald Grant for picture on p. 8 (top); Rex Features for picture on p. 5; Paramount Pictures Corp, courtesy Kobal for picture on p.2 (bottom), United Artists, courtesy Kobal on p.3 (top), Columbia, courtesy Kobal on p. 4 (bottom), Tri-Star, courtesy Kobal for picture on p. 6 (top).

Contents

Acknowledgements:

I was already established in Hollywood when John Travolta arrived in the mid-1970s. I've followed his career, through interviews, his movies, the scuttlebutt of Tinseltown watering holes, the gossip columns and the trade papers ever since. Often it was what Travolta did not say or do that proved most informative. Of course, over two decades there are scores of people to thank, which I do. In the past year the Hollywood film community and intimates who witnessed Travolta rise again with *Pulp Fiction, Get Shorty, Broken Arrow, Phenomenon* and *Michael* have all been agreeable and helpful. Travolta himself has never – even in the difficult days – shied away from questions or controversy in interviews, be it claims that he is gay or his membership of the Church of Scientology.

Of course there are always shades of emphasis and different perceptions, but I believe those who have spoken to me have tried to paint an honest picture of him. Travolta himself enjoys releasing little secrets, like revealing that he lost his virginity in 1968 at the age of fourteen and laughingly justifying: 'Hey, there was a sexual revolution going on.'

For the opportunity to tell the *full* story for the first time thanks to Charlie Carman at Boxtree.

As always, extraordinary special thanks to literary agent Judith Chilcote.

Foreword

False Idols

'If you listen to all the clowns around, you're just dead'

James Cagney's career advice to John Travolta

A s the 20th century marches to a conclusion – or totters, stumbles, or wanders, depending on individual circumstances – the horizon, as always, seems endless for Hollywood. Not Technicolor blue but rather more dollar green. With more worldwide satellites, channels and viewers come demands, demands, *demands!* The order is supply, supply, *supply!*

In 20th, going on 21st, century Hollywood a wartime environment exists, albeit with the officers wearing designer outfits and the generals wielding cheque books. The soldiers – the stars – are celluloid fodder. And the movie business is just as brutal and lethal as cannon. Win or perish.

Today you are not as good as your last movie. You are only as good as your last movie's opening weekend. If a big-budget, star-name film plays Friday evening through Sunday midnight without earning more than $10 million in American cinemas it is a flop. And a belly flop at that.

Yes, big names get even more money to move on from one failure to another but finally the merry millions-go-round game ends. It's like a lottery: everyone knows how to play, no one knows how to win. In our times of hollow celebrity and media frenzy there are many morality tales and victims in a one-industry town which builds idols only to casually break them down with disdain and often derision. Hollywood Babylon, indeed.

Sometimes Hollywood stars – be they actors, directors, writers or producers – collude in their own demise. Disillusionment is savage.

John Travolta has grown up and matured during some intense warfare and has beaten, it seems, the heartless Hollywood that creates and buries its own. Resurrection is no big Tinseltown trick – even a clumsy storyline can do that – but reviving a career is harder. That's a real miracle. Some stay dead, others reinvent themselves. Sylvester Stallone, for example, struggles on, announcing in 1996 that he aims to take on more acting than action roles. The multi-multi-millions of dollars have lost their attraction.

Perhaps it was not ego, but common sense that convinced Stallone to reconsider his career direction. Certainly, films like *Judge Dredd* in 1995 and *Assassins* in 1996 were short on thrills on screen and at the box office. Career longevity may come elsewhere.

Bruce Willis has proved that. A made-from-television superstar with the big bang shoot 'em up *Die Hard* films he has also worked in an alternative zone with films like *In Country*, *Nobody's Fool*, *Billy Bathgate*, Terry Gilliam's *Twelve Monkeys* and even more notably against type in Quentin Tarantino's *Pulp Fiction*. He has cleverly and successfully hedged his not inconsiderable multi-million dollar bets. Because if the star is big enough it is he or she who calls the shots. They are the ones who pick the movies – the script, the director and the co-stars. The opportunities for everything from pushing too hard to megalomania are as endless as that future horizon.

Gender is no shield from hazard: Julia Roberts' career took off with *Pretty Woman* in 1990 but she has not had a proper success since. Her almost-straight-to-video demise in the title role of the 1996 reworking of the Jekyll and Hyde story *Mary Reilly* followed other career misadventures in seemingly box-office-proof material, such as the film adaptation of superseller author John Grisham's *The Pelican Brief* and Steven Spielberg's *Hook*. In a matter of movies she was being written off.

As was Demi Moore, who was pilloried for the 1996 adaptation of Nathaniel Hawthorne's classic *The Scarlet Letter*. It was such a hugely publicised disaster that instead of the 'A' for adulteress she was forced to wear, they could have plastered a giant 'F' for flop over her enhanced and much revealed breasts. She had not enjoyed a blockbuster success since *Ghost* in 1990 ($217.6 million), but in the same year that *The Scarlet Letter* failed, she became the highest paid actress in the world. She was paid $12.5 million for her role as stripper Erin in *Striptease*, an adaptation of best-selling Miami author Carl Hiaasen's novel. Critics suggested that having ruined 19th-Century author Hawthorne's material she had gone contemporary to do the same for Hiaasen. A British magazine went so far as to announce the arrival of *Striptease* in cinemas with the headline 'The Bitch is Back'.

The pressure on stars is undoubtably exceptional and there is almost nothing anyone can do about it, except hang on. John Travolta did just that. He made some movies he shouldn't have made, but even when he appeared in box-office successes like *Look Who's Talking* he was largely criticised or ignored. He tried singing and dancing. He tried Pinter. He worked in theatre. He made a movie with a kid and a dog, and another with a cute girl whom he later married.

But he stuck at it long enough for Quentin Tarantino to arrive on the film scene and provide the *Pulp Fiction* potion, which brought Travolta suddenly and spectacularly back to box-office life. No one knows why the magic worked that time.

Travolta has always been fully confident of his abilities and strength. He has never seemed overly concerned about career mishaps or choices and apparently takes it all with a shrug: 'I was probably less preoccupied with my career than others were.'

His idol was James Cagney, a self-created, self-reliant actor-hoofer, who for so many years dominated the industry with his punchy personality. When asked for advice by a young Travolta, Cagney told him, 'Start with one thing: they need you. Without you they have an empty screen. So when you get on there just do what you think is right and stay with it. If you listen to all the clowns, you're just dead.'

According to the ageing star's longtime companion Marge Zimmermann, Travolta was 'like a little kid' around his hero. She said he was timid, almost child-like in attitude and speech. The boy/man who adored Cagney called him 'Jamesy'.

Jamesy Cagney? Oh, come on! But the perpetual Travolta charm worked. Cagney – *Mister* Cagney to most people – was fond of and helpful to the young actor who had sought him out. 'He was the *only* one outside of my family who was an inspiration to me,' Travolta said later.

And he absorbed all that Cagney had to say. Well, almost all. Travolta would listen to some of the clowns. But only *some*.

Prologue
The Lazarus Syndrome

'Movie star charisma made Travolta's screen resurrection inevitable.' The Hollywood 'bible', *Daily Variety*, 1996

The heavy draws on a couple of smuggled Havana cigars provided the only moments of light in the darkened front row of one of the most powerful screening rooms in Hollywood. The three men had been unusually silent during their first look at a highly touted new movie. As the film flickered to a conclusion they eased out of their seats and stretched.

Robert Evans flicked at a button by his chair and the overhead lights beamed on. Warren Beatty smiled slowly. As usual he was hesitant to be first with a verdict. Jack Nicholson had no qualms and with his huge grin announced to Evans,

'He'll be gigantic.'

'What's his name again?' asked Beatty.

Evans in his trademark yellow cashmere sweater and white tuxedo shirt beamed '*That* is John Travolta.'

'Oh, yeah, the kid from the TV series,' said Beatty, who two decades later would turn down the lead in a movie called *Get Shorty* because he didn't think audiences would believe in someone as handsome as he playing the leading role of a Miami loan shark.

But this was October 1977, and Beatty and every other actor in Hollywood would have sold their soul or their plastic surgeon to be in John Travolta's high-stepping dancing shoes.

The three friends had just seen an advance screening of *Saturday Night Fever*, the movie that made Travolta a star and the Robert Evans-controlled Paramount Studios millions of dollars. In the town where everyone wants to be a star and will do almost anything to achieve it, this was an important evening and the moment belonged to a kid from the New Jersey sticks.

Evans knew the score. He'd once been a beautiful kid in Hollywood too.

Hard left off the appropriately named Wonderland Avenue in the Hollywood Hills and around an intimidating driveway lies the gated 1910 French Regency estate of Evans, the legendary film producer and flamboyant *bon viveur*. Unlike its previous owner, Greta Garbo, the ebullient Evans never wants to be alone: his third ex-wife Ali MacGraw lives in a guest house and neighbours Warren Beatty and Jack Nicholson are regular visitors to a home that boasts a swimming pool with a centrepiece fountain comprising twenty-seven jets of water. The gardens and paved patio are overlooked by a Wimbledon-modelled tennis court.

It is a moment's drive from the centre of Beverly Hills and the world on which Evans has been gambling for more than four decades. He produced *Love Story* and *The Godfather* saga (in his patio garden is the cast iron black table where Brando signed the contract to star as Don Corleone) and other classics like Roman Polanski's *Chinatown* and *Rosemary's Baby*. He's also a Comeback Kid. Which is appropriate.

A Hollywood mogul, a success both in and out of the studio system, Evans was mugged by cocaine and an overcharged lust for life. The 1980s were professionally lost to him ('I earned about $10,000 and that was from a photograph of me that was used for an advertising campaign') but by the late 1990s he was back after two major movies and with the rights to a big-screen version of *The Saint* with former Batman, Val Kilmer, taking the Simon Templar role in the summer of 1996.

It was like old times. Friends around to stretch out in the comfortably cushioned screening room and watch the latest movies before they reached the world's cinemas. Just like it had been when Evans had the hot ticket to a sneak of *Saturday Night Fever*.

Evans recalls, 'When the movie ended the three of us just stared at the empty screen like we'd been hit by a truck. That kid Travolta was the sexiest male star we'd seen in years. We looked at each other and we were all thinking the same thing. It was Jack who said it first – how big Travolta would be.'

By the end of 1978 the young actor who, as a troubled teenager, had sought psychiatric help for depression could claim to be the greatest entertainer on the planet – not only the most wanted actor but a pop idol. Michael Eisner, who went on to become the boss of Disney and one of the most powerful figures in 1990s Hollywood, pronounced, 'He is the biggest star in the world, bar none. Just the mere fact that he is in a project – or *might* be in it – turns it into a major event.'

Travolta's name was added to the 1978 edition of *Who's Who in America*. He dined at the White House with President Jimmy Carter. He was on the cover of *Time* magazine (Menachem Begin and the turmoil in the Middle East managed a mention in the upper right corner of the magazine's cover) and over half a dozen pages he was compared to the legendary, sexually confused Montgomery Clift. Then, on 15 June 1978, *Rolling Stone* magazine put him on the cover and part of the editorial commentary read, 'He will be revered forever in the manner of Elvis, James Dean and Marilyn Monroe.'

True, he was never forgotten. But he was lost for a long time until stardom struck again with *Pulp Fiction* in 1994.

There was a homage to his *Pulp* dance with Uma Thurman in the 1996 film *Mr Holland's Opus* and a similar tribute in an episode of the internationally popular television hospital series *ER*. When Kurt Russell won a $15 million pay packet for the 1996 action movie *Executive Decision* his career leap was described throughout Hollywood as *Travoltaesque*.

Travolta has become an integral part of Hollywood, of film language. 'I think he just has such a presence on the screen that he's a convincing star and people rediscover him,' thinks Pauline Kael, the doyenne of American film critics. 'His youthfulness is intact in his face. He has a wonderfully expressive face.'

Only a few months after the screening at Wonderland Avenue, on Monday, 12 April 1978, Travolta was a Best Actor nominee and presenter at the Academy Awards. Looking just as nervous standing on the stage of the Dorothy Chandler Pavilion in downtown Los Angeles, as he did at the 1996 Oscars, he blurted to the applauding celebrity audience and millions of television viewers worldwide, 'It's a thrill to be just standing here.'

But in the 70s John Travolta was winning. At the age of twenty-four he had his Oscar nomination for his portrayal of Tony Manero, the hottest dancer at Brooklyn's 2001 Odyssey Club in *Saturday Night Fever*. The title is not even up on the screen when we see Travolta strutting and bopping down the street, each step stamping out his authority. Act? The actor taught to dance by Gene Kelly's brother Fred was back home in the town he described as 'hardly any place at all'. He hadn't even said a word, but that was the moment he became a superstar. *Grease* – the most successful movie musical ever – was waiting in the box-office wings. Stardom had seldom arrived so fast.

'It was all so amazing. The *excessiveness* of it all,' says Travolta. 'The weird thing is I thought *Saturday Night Fever* was just going to be a stepping stone. We did the movie thinking it would be a small art film. I don't know how to figure it. Was it the dancing? Was it the character? Was it the drama or the comedy? *What* was it?'

Whatever it was, somewhere they opened up a vault and the money poured in. Nearly two decades later Travolta, happily, says, 'I had a very clever agent and lawyer in those days who, working together, got me points [percentages] early on. It was the films and the soundtracks of *Saturday Night Fever, Grease, Urban Cowboy* and *Staying Alive* which made the money. Believe it or not, all those added up to way over a billion dollars.'

Money never mattered again. In 1995 he filmed *White Man's Burden* with Harry Belafonte for a modest $150,000 while his pay for John Woo's *Face Off* in 1997 would be close to $20 million.

Burden preceded his public renaissance but that was not the reason for the small fee. The film's budget dictated that. It was a project Travolta believed in and wanted to be involved with, a futuristic film set in a world where blacks and whites in America have exchanged roles, switched status. Travolta is a blue-collar worker wrongly sacked from his job who gets into crime to feed his family. If the film faltered, Travolta delivered. He and the American critics were pleased with his work, which mattered more than the dollars.

'Obviously, I vary my value. I'll do a film for nothing or I'll do a film for money depending on what the situation is. I just think it is a good indicator of the quality of script that might fall on your plate. I look at it like that because money has never been a particular problem or situation for me. It's not that I need to look for the big buck but, rather, does the big buck reflect that I'll get the first choice to nab the best stuff?

'It's more about clout. Money isn't necessarily an end; it's a by-product. But the opportunity and quality of work you get can actually be more satisfying.'

Travolta is a financial wiseguy and that, of course, has helped him retain the purity of his attitude to money: 'I kept a decent income coming in. A couple of my friends who had money for generations had said that you should target yourself to live off your interest. They told me that in 1978; those were the seeds that were planted and I never forgot them. I never want to work my whole life and then have someone take it away. I'd rather *spend* it.

'I watched people I knew take really big risks and some lost at it. I'm willing to do that with my career as an actor but not with money.'

His former girlfriend Marilu Henner, who found fame in *Taxi* and as Burt Reynolds' wisecracking wife in the 1990s' television success *Evening Shade*, has remained close since those first big-money days. 'Johnny's made more from those early films than from almost anything else. He's good with money. A lot of big stars waste it on stupid things but he really invests well.'

But did he invest well in his career? The distinguished critic David Thomson, author of *The Biographical Dictionary of Film*, believes that Travolta slammed into a narcissistic phase in that early storm of fame: 'He became a street dandy so dedicated to impressing people that he bypassed self-knowledge. His is the face of a heavy, swollen passion brought on by mirror-gazing.'

Thomson thought that Travolta would never return to the heights of yesteryear but admitted in 1996, 'I have certainly been proved wrong. I thought he was gone. And while I am pleased for him, I am certainly surprised by that.'

Travolta indulged himself. He had plenty of time – and money – to spend in the 1980s as his career floundered. He bought homes (in California, Florida, Maine), cars (Mercedes, Jaguar, a 1995 Chevrolet convertible) and planes (a Lear jet, a World War II era Vampire and, more recently, a Gulfstream 11) on the back of his hat-trick of young male 'attitude' movies, *Fever, Grease* and *Urban Cowboy*. At the same time he rejected films like *Arthur* (Dudley Moore's giant hit), *Splash* (the movie that made Tom Hanks a star) and *Midnight Express* (superstar director Oliver Stone's first Oscar as screenwriter). Also lost were Terence Malick's elegiac *Days of Heaven* (Richard Gere's big-screen debut), *American Gigolo* and *An Officer and a Gentleman* (all films that established Gere, who played the lead in the 1973 London stage production of *Grease*, as a Hollywood star) as well as *Prince of the City* which Brian De Palma, who had directed Travolta in the 1976 film *Carrie* and *Blow Out* in 1981, was developing.

That other 1990s wonderboy, Quentin Tarantino, says that the moment when Travolta lost *Prince of the City* in 1981 (Treat Williams won the role) was one of the most upsetting for him in the history of the cinema. 'That's the movie. If I had to make a list of five movies that were never made that I would cry tears for, that's one of the five!'

Tarantino was never going to allow Travolta to reject *Pulp Fiction*, the violent anthem to love and honour, murder and mayhem in and on the far side of Los Angeles, which he had written and would direct. It took some talking.

According to Travolta the writer-director gave it to him full blast. 'Quentin said, "What did you *do*? Don't you remember what Pauline Kael said about you ['his willingness to go emotionally naked was equal to Brando's']? What Truffaut said about you ['the greatest American actor of his time']? Don't you know what you mean to the American cinema? John, what did you *do*?"

'I was hurt – but moved. He was telling me I had promise like no one else's. I went out there with my tail between my legs. I was devastated. I couldn't find the words. But I also thought, "Jesus Christ, I must have been a fucking good actor".'

Desperate as Tarantino was to cast Travolta in *Pulp Fiction* there were obstacles for him with the film company Miramax. But the greatest hurdle was Travolta's image: the *Saturday Night Fever* stereotype.

'The whole teeny bopper/disco stigma weighed John down tremendously. Even if you did like him at a certain point in the 1980s you couldn't admit to it,' said Tarantino. 'You weren't just talking about an actor. You were talking about a figurehead for something that was despised – disco.

'Miramax would do these little office polls where they would ask secretaries, "What do you think of John Travolta?" And they'd say, "Him? Oooh. Yuck!". I was just holding on and saying, "Fuck all you guys". '

Travolta was paid $140,000 for *Pulp Fiction*. It was the best deal of his career. His answer to all the 'bad choices' (a euphemism for flops) was and remains, 'You feel bad. You feel a loss. But give a guy the benefit of not being *insane*. Leave it at "bummed out". Disasters are earthquakes, airplane crashes, the *Titanic*. I'm sorry but a bad movie is not a disaster.'

His simple answer to all the *Pulp Fiction* questions is now the established, 'No movie has ever been that important to me.' Each time he says it, he means it. And every time he would appear to be more interested in his questioner's opinion. He retains that whispery, transparent quality that makes most people want to cheer for him. He explains part of it this way, 'I remember once approaching a star who shall remain nameless, when I was younger. I was shut out and it just killed me. I thought, "If I'm ever in that position, I'll never do that". '

He has always had discreet charm. From the moment he arrived in Hollywood he treated movie executives and fans with careful courtesy. Away from the cameras he appeared shy and apparently vulnerable . On screen he established himself as the slim, dark tough guy with glowing, knowing blue eyes and a clever haircut and smile. He filled the air with cigarette smoke and naughty words.

They said he walked like Cagney (his weight in the hips, shifting like gears), smouldered like Valentino, had the magnetic sensitivity of a young Brando, and they talked about him in the same sentences as James Dean and Elvis. But through good and bad times John Travolta has remained his own man. He has also matured in a town with no rules other than success. Without it you are nobody. Travolta has always been *somebody*. The image is of Mr Cool but it is a calculated veneer. The fire of ambition has always burned. Yes, it's flickered but it has never gone out.

As the millennium approaches, and he is arguably the most important movie star in the world, he reflects on his own rules: 'Always make your own decisions, never compromise your integrity; don't communicate unless you yourself want to communicate. I think living life you have to rub elbows with all sorts of people. You have to be willing to experience anything. And if you can try to live by those things you are going to have a shot at a better life than you would normally.' He is philosophical about his rollercoaster decades as a star and well aware of all the hurdles where others have fallen: 'Normally, a guy like me is dead by now, one way or another. Let's face it.'

He is a positive thinker. He's had to be. He has been a devoted Scientologist for nearly two decades and says that the teachings have helped him through personal tragedies he found much more hurtful than any career 'disaster'.

He retains that magic which so enthused Robert Evans and his cohorts in the darkened Wonderland Avenue screening room. For millions just hearing the Bee Gees pounding out 'Stayin' Alive' conjures up the image of John Travolta, all macho man puffed up with carnal knowledge.

After romantic encounters with women ranging from French enchantress Catherine Deneuve to all-American Brooke Shields, he finally married actress Kelly Preston in September 1991. His son Jett was born seven months later.

Shortly after buying his Gulfstream 11, Travolta – a graduate of American Airlines' flight school for jet pilots in Texas – was co-piloting the plane into Washington, D.C. His wife and son were in the passenger seats. Approaching the American capital the plane lost power and instruments going through a cloud bank.

'That was almost a disaster. But it's like, "Hey, I almost got mugged today." What does it really mean?

'When you fly a plane you buy into the idea that it's dangerous fare and that you'll do the best job to have it not be. But you don't like tying others into that play. So I thought: "God, for the first time in twenty-three years' flying, why does it have to be a time when my family's on board?"

'On the other hand, maybe it gave me that higher sense of survival and protectivism because of them. Man, I was cool as ice.

'Everyone thinks I'm cool on screen, but me in that cockpit – that was cool.'

He had to stay that way because Hollywood had the hots for him.

Chapter One
A Star is Reborn

'**Look at me!**' John Travolta as loan shark

turned Hollywood film producer Chili Palmer in *Get Shorty*, 1996, at the 1996

Golden Globe Awards.

The rain coming in from the Pacific had been backed up all the way to Japan for days and by early Sunday afternoon, on 21 January 1996, the long red carpet stretching from the limousine drop-off point to the entrance of the Beverly Hilton Hotel was sodden. Shoes squelched as the crowds outside and in the doorway of the hotel cheered, while the paparazzi elbowed camera-clicking tourists for an image of the celebrities arriving for the 53rd Annual Golden Globe Awards.

In the 1990s the Globes, given by the Hollywood Foreign Press Association (HFPA) and once disdained, if not by the stars at least by their agents and advisers, had become a strong predictor of the Academy Awards. It is no coincidence that they always precede the Oscar nominations – in 1996 the Oscar ballots closed on 1 February just ten days after the Globe awards – and promotion-hungry stars and studios offer full support, hoping in return for an award season boost.

For John Travolta – once again the king of Hollywood – the awards were no chore. As he put on his Armani tux in the master bedroom of the $25,000-a-month Beverly Hills home he and Kelly were renting only a short drive from the Hilton, even the torrential rain could not dampen his spirits.

What had irritated him was his wardrobe of half a dozen tuxedos: 'I have a hard time figuring out which pants go with which jacket. If you hang them separately you can't match them up. They're all black but they're not all the same.' Finally, his Valentino black tie straightened, he was ready for the Starlite limousine waiting on Alpine Drive and for the awards given by the eighty-three HFPA members with whom he had long been popular and friendly.

'But being popular with us is not a guarantee of an award,' warned the organisation's treasurer Jack Tewksbury, adding, 'It's all judged on the movie and the performance. Often your heart might press you to vote for a favourite star but your brain tells you that another performance is the one that must win.'

The Globe voters have one advantage over their 6,463 Academy Award counterparts. They offer the Globe statuettes in two categories. So, for example, Travolta was nominated for *Get Shorty* as Best Actor in a Musical or Comedy and Nicolas Cage was up for *Leaving Las Vegas* as Best Actor in a Drama.

Cage won and followed up with the Best Actor Oscar on 27 March. Travolta also won but was shut out of the Oscar nominations. Cage, Sean Penn (*Dead Man Walking*), Richard Dreyfuss (*Mr Holland's Opus*), Massimo Troisi (*Il Postino*) and Anthony Hopkins (*Nixon*) were the 1996 nominees.

It was an unexpected exclusion. Although *Get Shorty* director Barry Sonnenfeld stands by the cruel rule of Hollywood that everyone wants you to fail, he believes Travolta was the exception in 1996: 'Industry screenings are always the worst. People want to give you the thumbs down. But ours was unbelievable. People were interrupting it to applaud John. They want John to succeed. The reason's simple: the industry needs movie stars and John is one.'

Travolta certainly looked the part at the Golden Globes alongside a happy Mel Gibson (a big winner for *Braveheart*), Sharon Stone (Best Actress for *Casino*), Emma Thompson with her Best Screenplay award for *Sense and Sensibility* and Sean Connery with his special Cecil B. de Mille Award.

Travolta wore his trademark grin with his perfectly matched tuxedo as he accepted his honour and said to the cheering audience: 'You've given me faith and at the risk of sounding like a cliche – look at me!'

His thanks included an acknowledgement of Scientology founder L. Ron Hubbard. He is acutely aware of the negative reaction to such comments – and his motivation has been questioned – but he is not concerned.

Some weeks later, he explained: 'I feel about Hubbard the way I feel about my manager and family and co-actors: he helped me. It's so clear to me that I wouldn't be where I am without the insights and help I got through Scientology. Between the ages of eighteen and twenty I was on a very self-destructive path. I want to acknowledge Hubbard as others would thank their managers… or a film studio head.'

He also shrugged off his omission from the Oscar nominee list, laughing, 'I figure I'm in good company.' He pointed to others who had missed out: his friend Tom Hanks (*Apollo 13*), fellow Scientologist Nicole Kidman (*To Die For*), Jennifer Jason Leigh (*Georgia*) and director Ang Lee (*Sense and Sensibility*), saying, 'A lot of people thought the quality of their movies would be good enough but it doesn't work that way'.

But Travolta was working regularly and his interest in what he was doing matched the ongoing reaction to him. 'When we were shooting *Get Shorty* there were girls on the street screaming: " Johnnnnn…Johnnn!!…Johnn."

'It was the *Hard Day's Night* scream,' recalls his co-star Rene Russo. 'And it was amazing because it wasn't all forty-year-old Travolta fans. These were teenagers.'

This was the youthful enthusiasm of his early television days when *Welcome Back, Kotter* made him a teen idol. On 7 March 1996, he was named 'Male Star of the Year' by the cinema owners of America at the NATO/ShoWest celebrations in Las Vegas. That evening *Kotter* was on half a dozen US cable TV channels.

It was in Las Vegas that Joe Roth, chairman of the Walt Disney Motion Picture Group, spelled it out clearly: 'John is returning to the place where he was the biggest star in the business. He brings people in on the opening weekend and you can only say that about a handful of actors.' Tom Sherak of Twentieth Century Fox, which released *Broken Arrow* was just as enthusiastic: 'Travolta is as hot an actor as there is in today's marketplace. There is no one hotter.'

Travolta took advantage of the heat – and plans to continue doing so into the next century. His friend Jonathan Krane, who became his personal manager in 1985, sees nothing to stop him: 'He's always had unwavering confidence and the enduring belief that the right thing will happen. He's never defined himself by other people. That's very, very difficult to do in Hollywood. I think that John is one of the very few actors who can successfully play goofy comedy, sweet, regular guys, fascinating villains, cool guys – he can do all those things so interestingly. Our plans are to continue to find that diversity.

'This "comeback" tag is a distortion based on John's initial phenomenal success. See, John was an icon and so everything he did was measured in more drastic terms. It's amazing what's happened to him since *Pulp Fiction* but he's still the same Travolta. The qualities that come out when he acts are an aspect of his warmth and decency as a human being. He is always honest in his business and personal dealings.'

Naturally Krane, who is married to actress Sally *M*A*S*H* Kellerman, has his friend's and his own interests at heart. He was executive producer of the supernatural comedy *Michael*, which Travolta filmed on location in Austin, Texas, early in 1996. Guided by *Sleepless in Seattle* director Nora Ephron, the film co-stars Oscar-winner William Hurt and the ravishing Andie MacDowell. Of her title star Ephron said, 'He's totally sexual and completely innocent at the same time. It's hard to think of another American actor who has that combination and who, by the way, is very funny.'

The way Travolta tells it, his debauched angel Michael *sounds* funny. Taking a break from the location cameras he explained his role: 'I'm the archangel Michael who first appears on screen in a big pair of boxer shorts. He's a smoker, a womaniser and a drinker who loves sugar – especially chocolate cookies. He's a warrior, yes, but he has been through so many historical events that he's just thrashed. Even his wings are dirty.'

But Travolta was flying – Hollywood style.

During his dry years he had flown around the world, as Jonathan Krane was quick to point out: 'John never sat around the house waiting for the phone to ring. He'd fly his jets around the world. I'd get calls from him from Africa. He'd say, "Anything going on, Jon?" I'd say I hadn't gotten anything I liked and he'd say, "OK, call you in a few weeks." And then he'd go off. He always managed to please himself.'

Which Travolta was also doing in 1996: 'I'm so tired of saying no to good scripts and yes to time off that for the next five or six years I'd like to work as much as I can. Just because (a) I can, (b) I feel like it and (c) who knows when I'll have the opportunity again to get top level scripts? As far as I'm concerned I'm getting offered the best material in town so why not take it advantage of it? I certainly went through enough years without it. My father worked 52 weeks a year. Why shouldn't I?'

Before *Michael*, he had completed another fantasy film, *Phenomenon*. Travolta had been instantly attracted to it, joking, 'It's a phenomenal script – no, really, it's beautifully written. It's really about the heart. It goes into the *Forrest Gump* range to some degree.'

He plays an 'everyday guy', a petrol station attendant, who is suddenly struck by genius. Directed by Jon Turteltaub, who launched Sandra Bullock into the $10 million-a-film range with *When You Were Sleeping*, it was another notch on the 'new' Travolta career. Released in America in the summer of 1996 it was his first major warm-weather movie in years. And it was not a big comedy or an action adventure. But Disney believed that releasing Travolta on holiday America was no risk even at that crucial box-office time (more than 40 per cent of ticket sales are made during the period) and film president Donald De Line explained their confidence: 'We felt that in a crowded marketplace it stood out as something unique. We believed from the start that John was the perfect guy for the role. He played an Everyman to whom something extraordinary happens and we felt the audience would take that journey with him.'

De Line was boosted by the success of *Broken Arrow*, which Disney also backed. That film's director, John Woo, never had any concerns about casting Travolta. 'Action is easy. Anybody can do it. What I needed for *Broken Arrow* was a great, serious actor which is why I wanted him.' The Hong Kong director compares Travolta to his tougher-than-titanium action star, Asia's post-Modernist hero Chow Yun-Fat: 'His presence is the same, so natural and elegant.'

Travolta's first full-scale bad guy delighted audiences (some critics found him too nice) and Jonathan Krane: 'People are more than drawn to the characters John creates – they want to become them. John brings his own power into the film. It hasn't been directed into it. He reinvented the villain. He made a villain who is vulnerable, who has a heart. He's made it OK to be the bad guy.'

Certainly action-wizard Woo liked his star. In late 1996 he signed Travolta for

$20 million to co-star with that year's *Leaving Las Vegas* Oscar winner Nicolas Cage in the terrorist thriller *Face Off* for Paramount, which was anticipated as the major US summer movie of 1997.

Another event that year was to have been *The Double* but just before filming began in Paris in June 1996, Travolta abruptly flew home to America. Initially it was said by Travolta's people that he was concerned about his son's need for an ear operation, but that was only part of the story.

The Roman Polanski adaptation of the Dostoevsky novella was first offered to Jack Nicholson – it would have re-teamed him and Polanski for the first time since the landmark *Chinatown* in 1974 – but Nicholson had a scheduling conflict with another film. The project was taken to Sony Pictures-based Mandalay Entertainment from the New Regency Company by executive Adam Platnick.

Travolta had been interested in the film while New Regency had the rights but they could not agree on 'creative aspects' and his salary. When the Tinseltown merry-go-round stopped a year later he was offered $17 million plus lucrative inducements to guarantee more than $20 million. Travolta was to play Jake, an American accountant in Paris who believes a double – also played by Travolta – is taking over his identity.

Travolta was originally overwhelmed by the deal – and the chance to work with Polanski. But, as usual, he tried to be cool about his excitement: 'I negotiated to get paid twice as much. I got twice as many meal breaks and I asked for two trailers.' But he takes pains to let it be understood that he is aware of the chances he is getting, 'Even at my hottest point in the past I don't think I'd been offered more than three or four scripts a year, sometimes one a year…Now I don't have the time to read the amount of scripts that are coming in. I am totally, fully aware of how unusual and how full-bodied this experience is in terms of opportunity.'

A few weeks later Travolta explained why he had decided to walk away from *The Double*. As it turned out his son had not needed an ear operation after all, but it also emerged that he felt the film was no longer the one he had contracted to be involved with: 'I signed to make one script, film A, and when I got to Paris they wanted me to make another film, film B. That was not what I contracted to do. I feel that at this stage in my career, I want to be in control. I talk to my advisors, I go to Scientologist classes, but I make the decisions.'

Basking in strong reviews for Phenomenon and talking of plans to co-star with his wife late in 1997, Travolta had no qualms about his decision to leave Paris: 'I walked away from millions of dollars which I would have liked, but also from a script I didn't like'. He speaks with assurance, with a confidence that gets noticed.

That icy stare, that 'Look at me!', that Travolta taught Danny DeVito in *Get*

Shorty also gets attention. Twentieth Century Fox bought Douglas Richardson's novel *Dark Horse* and it is being developed as a film vehicle for Travolta and his friend, actor turned director Ron *Apollo 13* Howard. Richardson's novel was anticipated as a major bestseller on publication in January 1997, and the follow-up movie a major investment for Fox. The political thriller set in Texas involves a *Mr Smith Goes To Washington* idealist up against a charming psychopath for a US Congressional seat. Both film and book involve more action than political debate.

Travolta was still deciding in the summer of 1996 whether to play the good or bad guy in the project – the producers gave him the choice of either role. Brian Grazer, who owns Imagine Films with Ron Howard said, 'Ron and I have known John since 1981 when we wanted him to do *Splash* and it didn't work out. We've wanted to work with him ever since.'

Of course, all these years later, so did everyone else.

'He's the guy,' said Miramax president Harvey Weinstein. And in case we missed the point he gushes, 'He can do anything. Villain, good guy, bad guy, medium-sized guy, romantic guy – he's gone beyond being a superstar, which he was in the first incarnation, and become a brilliant actor. Olivier, Tracy, Newman – there are very few guys you can say that about. He's there, man.'

Jon Turteltaub was equally enthusiastic: 'I would say that John Travolta is somewhere between Cary Grant and Shirley Temple. He has that child-like charm and the guy can sing and dance but he's also a very sexy man. But maybe he is more Jimmy Stewart because he has that Everyman quality. John loves to perform. In fact, there's a lot of Jimmy Cagney in him. When Cagney walked on screen you watched him. So, OK, maybe there's a Cagney–Mickey Rooney quality, only taller. I don't know. I'm just thrilled to death he's in my movie.'

Travolta has that effect. More composed, his director offered: 'I was expecting what my image of Travolta was: a very cool, hip, sexy, dark, romantic actor; what I got was an ebullient, silly, cuddly goofball.'

By the summer of 1996 there was talk of Travolta starring in a musical, and some serious name dropping: 'The next recording I do will be for a movie I'm also in. Maybe a musical. Maybe opposite Streisand since she and I seem to be the only two actors still interested in that genre. I've talked to Steven Spielberg about it. We'll see.'

The thought takes Travolta back to where the dancing began, in 1962 when he was eight years old. He acts the announcer part: 'Ladies and gentlemen, the Englewood Yearly Fireworks presents that dance craze, the twist, danced by little Johnny Travolta.'

Was he cool?

'*Sure.*'

Chapter Two
Little Johnny

'I can't imagine a world without my Johnny' John Travolta's mother Helen in 1978

John Travolta – always Johnny to his family – was the youngest of six children and spoiled rotten. His mother Helen saw it simply: 'Johnny's the baby. You're supposed to baby babies.'

He was an adventurer and entertainer from the start, and his mother's delight: 'I knew Johnny would become a performer even before he was born. He danced in my womb.'

She had ignored the criticism of family and friends (the tactless and the uncomprehending had called her 'stupid' to become pregnant with her sixth child at the age of 42) and in a family where they counted blessings more often than dollars she would tell everyone, 'I never expected a reward for bringing a baby into the world so late in my life. I took what God sent me. But if I'd listened to the people who said it was "disgusting" to have a child at my age I wouldn't have had Johnny. Now, I can't imagine the world without my Johnny.'

Her youngest son arrived four days after St Valentine's Day in February 1954, when she still had the 'anonymous' Valentine's Day cards from her other two sons and husband on display.

Her yelling new arrival was an attention-grabber from the start – mainly from doctors. His had been an easy birth but the first eighteen months were a continual worry. The baby caught all the neighbourhood bugs and colds. He ate well but was still frail. The local doctors all knew the way to the Travoltas' three-storey clapboard home, which was within sight of the George Washington Bridge, at 135 Morse Place, Englewood, New Jersey.

The family house was on a tree-lined street in a substantial suburban town (pop: 27,000) just twenty minutes away from New York. In Manhattan the skyscrapers pointed like fingers to the future while back in Englewood the Travolta family were rooted in their past.

Family and tradition were always important to John's father, Salvatore Travolta.

The son of Sicilian and Neapolitan immigrants, he was one of four brothers who learned that sharing was a part of growing up. His father worked in garages and finally was able with his brothers to open a second-hand tyre 'emporium' in the years before World War I. It was a time when the poor of Europe were arriving by the shipload, everyone looking for work, and to establish a business so quickly was quite an achievement. His mother worked in a nearby garment factory on exploitive wages.

This was the land of opportunity where everybody could be anything they wanted. A prince or a president. It was to become something of a motto for the Travolta family that goals were important and that achieving them was never impossible, just a matter of time and effort. You got nothing for nothing. You worked for it. You waited for it.

Salvatore Travolta was seventeen years old when he met Helen Burke, also seventeen, the independent, at times aloof, daughter of Irish-English parents, at a charity dance in their home town of Hackensack, New Jersey. She was dark and stunning and everyone, except her domineering mother Aileen, told her she should be an actress. Salvatore – 'Dut' to his family and close friends, Sam to everyone else – was a local star, a college athlete, scholarship American footballer and a baseball whiz. From the moment she was walking and talking Helen Burke had been a performer; she had always wanted to make an impression. But when her youngest son became a worldwide star she never gloried in it: she was happy for him and hopeful for him but she wanted it to last.

His parents' relationship and lives dominated John Travolta's life. It has been the hardest act he has had to follow. His parents forsook what might have been for what was to make them eternally happy and thankful. Their son maintains, 'My father should have been a big, big professional athlete and my mother should have been Bette Davis. She would have been Davis or Barbara Stanwyck, he would have been Lombardi [US football legend Vince Lombardi], you know what I mean? They had that drive. They were a hot couple.She was the beautiful Irish actress and he was the Cary Grant athlete.

'I had a wonderful, happy childhood and so did my brothers and sisters. I think my parents liked to inspire creativity, winningness, productivity in their children. Whatever you were interested in is what they celebrated for you. If you wanted them to be at your basketball game or come down to the basement and watch you perform a show, that's what they did. It mattered to them what we thought, felt and did, our happiness being so important to them that they were almost selfless in how big a deal it was. I could always express my feelings to them and they could say almost anything to me. The love was there. Still is, really.

'As I got older, I realised how rare my parents were. From the time I was five years old I talked with them as if they were my friends. The most poignant thing about them is that they never had any resentment about not having the careers they might have but for us. Their job was having these children. I feel so fortunate to have had them as parents.'

Writer Barbara Grizzuti Harrison became close to Travolta's mother and remembers, 'She loved all her children and her love and approval was not contingent upon their success or fame. She was a modest, gallant woman and John loved – loves – those qualities. Once she told me a story about how she swam across the Hudson River setting a long distance swimming record. It was no mean accomplishment. "Why is your hair wet?" her mother asked her. "Because I swam across the river," she said. Her mother told her: "Go dry your hair!" It was hardly an enthusiastic response.'

'Her mother never validated her efforts or her dreams,' says John Travolta talking of the grandmother he never knew. 'But my mother transcended her as only a large soul could. Some people if they are badly parented take it out on their own kids. Not my mom. At the Academy Awards when I was up for *Saturday Night Fever* I heard her say to my dad, "I'm glad Johnny didn't win." At first I didn't understand. I asked my father why she said that. "She said she wanted you to have something to look forward to," he said. She didn't need the gratification – and she was dying. She wanted me to be more than a one-movie star.'

As a teenager all Helen Burke wanted was to be Mrs Salvatore Travolta and have 'lots and lots of kids'. She had been to Columbia University, studied drama, produced, directed plays and acted (insisting on using her professional name, Helen Burke) and her boyfriend had completed college and his athletic career and had invested in a Firestone Tyre Company franchise (the Travolta Tire Exchange in Hillsdale, New Jersey) before they finally married in 1937. It was the year Bette Davis began her decade as Hollywood's box-office queen and James Cagney was about to go to the electric chair in *Angels with Dirty Faces*. The bride and groom were both twenty-six, and hopelessly happy. For Sam Travolta this was what life was all about. Decades later he would say that when the waiting was over it was all birthdays from then on. Life had become a partnership. Hugs not diamonds, they used to laugh, were forever. Marriage intoxicated them but it didn't make them rash.

They had waited to be prudent. In post-Depression America there were still fears that you could put down foundations for the future and watch them cave in. But there had never been and never would be anyone else for either of them. It was a love story they lived out for their children.

'I'll tell you again my father looked like Cary Grant and my mom like Barbara

Stanwyck – they were both more beautiful than any of their children,' said John Travolta adding – and this was in 1996 – quite seriously, 'Including me.'

Mr and Mrs Travolta set up their home in Morse Place – Sam Travolta's rocking chair in the corner of the living room, the big, intimidating oak dining table with its crocheted cloth in the centre – and began making plans to keep the doctors and midwives at Englewood Hospital busy. Ellen arrived in 1940, Sam Junior in 1944, Margaret in 1946, Annie in 1949 and Joey – thought to be the last of the Morse Place Gang – in 1952. When 'little Johnny' joined the family two years later his mother cried, 'I am blessed.' Her husband hugged her and said, 'I am a satisfied man.'

In the spring of 1996, himself a father, John Travolta could better understand his father's satisfaction. Sam Travolta Senior had pronounced of his family, 'Once we had those kids, my life became unimportant. Theirs were the important lives.' His son reflected, 'Life began when his children were born. He felt that prior to that it seemed – not that it didn't exist – but it seemed so much less important to him.'

Sam Travolta Senior, by the late 70s balding, a little paunchy and cigar-smoking (he joked that his kids, not pasta, had stolen his athletic figure) was a contented man before his youngest son became a superstar. He was always pleased with all his children. 'We let our kids do pretty much what they wanted to do. "You want to go out? OK, you don't have to tell me where you're going or when you'll be home – just don't get into any trouble".'

'All my kids got jobs as soon as they could. I had a tyre shop. It didn't bring a lot of money. They knew we didn't have much and they didn't want to be burdens. Johnny was working in a supermarket when he was thirteen. Our daughter Margaret made good money – $100 a week – as a waitress. She gave ten dollars to Helen and ten dollars to me. And she knew she had to share with the little ones too.

'Margaret would slap a couple of dollars in front of Johnny and say: "Here, you brat!" She loved the brat.'

In the 1990s the Travoltas were still close, getting together for family celebrations, for Christmas and holidays. Their parents had planned it that way. Their father had said: 'Helen and I made up our minds we'd be home for our kids. We believe kids don't forget.

'I don't think I spent more than ten days out at night all the time the kids were growing up. My own mother and father were always home when we came back from school. I never forgot how important it was to me to know they were always there...'

Home was familiar. Little changed. The family dog Bootsie, a mongrel with bad teeth and an appetite for anything, had gnawed around an antique Czechoslovakian chest but it stayed on display. Photographs of the children hung alongside a still life of roses painted by Helen's father. Sam's rocking chair, like the dining room table, stayed in the same place for forty-one years. At one time or another he rocked all his children to sleep in it.

'Johnny would come home, sit in my lap and put his arm around my neck and say, "What do you think, Dad? Am I doing good? Do you think I'm making the right decisions?"'

'We wanted the kids home as much as they could do it. When they were growing up I used to buy hot dogs for everybody and the neighbourhood kids came to this yard. I built them a bowling alley down in the cellar. They played with plastic balls and old bottles. Johnny used to invite them down to play for two cents a game. He bought a five-cent soda and sold it for ten cents. Any kid who knocked down ten bottles got ten free sodas – only nobody could do it!'

By 1996 the trees had vanished from Morse Street and, to John Travolta's eyes, it just wasn't the same. 'It was all those naked homes there which really was unfortunate. Now, it looks like some sci-fi film. I can't even correlate it to my memories.'

When his son's first burst of fame hit, the usually implacable Sam Travolta thought that not just the trees but his comfortable, bric-a-brac stuffed home and most of the neighbourhood was coming down. The *Saturday Night Fever* fans arrived like locusts. 'They nibbled at the house as if it was made of gingerbread. The shingles were prised loose, plastic flowers were taken from the porch – they were after anything Johnny's hand might have touched. Anything removable went. They meant no harm. I wasn't complaining. Johnny always said: " Pa, please don't sell the house. I need a place to come home to." If we'd auctioned off the house bit by bit we'd have probably made a million. "John Travolta Slept Here." '

But home was more than a house with Americana furnishings and a clutter of photographs. It was all about old-style values. You helped other people; loyalty was not a casual thing and you never forgot your friends. Certainly you never forgot your family. In the evenings Sam and Helen would sit around talking about the old days. When he was fourteen John Travolta bought a double-breasted grey suit, a black shirt and a white tie for eighteen dollars at a New Jersey store. Somewhere he still has a picture of himself posing with a toy machine gun alongside his sister Margaret, who was dressed like Faye Dunaway in *Bonnie and Clyde* - the violent, controversial movie hit of the time.

That evening his father told him about his grandfather. He had worked long, eighteen-hour days and at one time had enough money – just twenty-five dollars but a lot of money in those distant days – to buy suits for his four sons. He pondered about it. Finally, the decision was made and the money went to a cousin who was on hard times and living in filth in a broken-down apartment building in New York.

Travolta's brother Joey lives in affluent Tarzana in California's suburban San Fernando Valley. Hollywood, where he works in film and music production, is a forty-minute drive away. His wife Wendy teaches computer classes at Castlemont School near their rambling five-bedroomed Spanish-style home. They have two children and are another Travolta happy family. Joey recalls his parents with deep affection. His father had 'innate dignity and charm – Italian presence and charisma.' He recalled the growing-up days: 'There were always hugs and kisses. They were always there, always protective. I learned from my Ma that you may have to deal with people who aren't nice but you don't have to be like them.

'And I learned from my father that you can deal with anybody and just be yourself. If Johnny and I have one thing in common besides the good things our parents gave us it's that we're street-wise. Johnny and I went to a tough school. The best actors come from the streets, not from Hollywood studios. That's why home was – still is in an emotional way – important to us.

'Johnny was the baby – and what an appetite! Johnny ate more junk food than any living person. He had a love affair with Mars bars. But it never seemed to make him fat – he was always thin. He was all bones. It didn't stay that way as he got older. Johnny isn't like anybody else. He's versatile – he can stretch to do any part. He was always acting around the house or ducking off to the basement to put on shows. He'd play act the stuff that Ma had taken him to see.'

Helen regularly presented plays in high schools in the area and also taught drama at Englewood High. She worried that 'little Johnny' would be lonely – his brothers and sisters were at school and the offspring of other families on Morse Place were also older than him – so he was taken along to rehearsals. 'There weren't other youngsters around for him. He had to create his own entertainment. He looked into himself, he was creative. He was a lonely child,' said his mother. 'Johnny matured quickly and at the age of four expressed an interest in acting.

'I knew about performance [she'd been one of the trio of 'Sunshine Sisters' on a local radio station in the early 1930s] and I'd acted in a repertory company. They used to call me Barbara Stanwyck. I told Johnny that once you become a character you are another person. You have to be quiet when it is not your turn. And you don't just make an entrance by running into a room. You let people have a look at you as you walk in.'

He never forgot – *Look at me!*

Chapter Three

Bumps and *Grind*

'He changed into one of my
wife's dresses for the stripper scene'

Sam Travolta on his youngest son's show-stopper

'Spotlight Johnny', his parents called him, for toddler John Travolta enjoyed putting on such an outrageous performance that he could not miss grabbing their attention.

All Helen Travolta's children had been given a glimpse of showbusiness and the benefits of her advice, her 'tips' as she called them. Ellen, the first born, was immediately bitten by her mother's contagious acting bug. John Travolta was six years old when he was taken to see his eldest sister in a road company production of *Gypsy*. She had a walk-on part and the star was the legendary Ethel *Call Me Madam* Merman. Ellen remembers her little brother being 'in awe' of everything about the show, the theatre itself and most of all 'the acting'. She recalled: 'He jumped from his own make-believe world right into ours. He seemed to have found his home. He'd mouth all Merman's songs and he could dance every part.'

Half a dozen years later he spent a school holiday on the road with his sister and *Gypsy*. He spent his time backstage and learning all the songs and dances. But the young, spellbound fan had to settle for make-believe at home...

'Sam had bought a record of the show for him and he played music from *Gypsy* all the time,' his mother would recall, adding, 'He sang and danced all the parts, male and female. He dragged all the dress-up clothes from my costume trunk. He was tremendous, even then. But he was shy. He'd act and sing and dance in the basement so none of the older kids would catch him at it. When my other children were away at school Johnny would say: "Ma, let's play-act".'

His father always fondly remembered the *Gypsy* evenings: 'He mimed the songs on the record and played all the parts. He wore an old tuxedo with the trousers rolled up so he wouldn't trip over them. Then, he changed into one of my wife's dresses for the stripper scene. My wife had trunks and trunks of old costumes down in the cellar and he'd use them to rehearse all the parts, the men's parts *and* the women's parts. Everyone from the newsboys to the chorus dancers. He memorised all their roles. Then, when he was ready, he would invite my wife and me down to see his little show. But he would *never* let the kids see this. His brothers and sisters teased him a lot.

'See, Johnny was real skinny and his older brother Joey gave him a nickname, "Bone". I'd come home from work and Joey, who was always cracking jokes, would say to me in front of Johnny: "Hey, Dad, what's left of a chicken after all the meat is gone." And I'd laugh and say: "Why, the bone." Johnny would get very upset and hurt thinking that Joey and I were making fun of him.'

The fledgling entertainer – oblivious to any dubious connotations to performing in drag – was able to bump and grind up a storm. He had already perfected the hand movements for the twist he would use decades later in *Pulp Fiction*. He had the moves, the presence, from the start. His mother, who had watched all her children flirt with the entertainment business always felt 'this is the one'. And, being the 'baby' his seemed like a special blessing for her because it was her last chance at stardom as well.

And, in a way, her son was her. She'd taught him and protected him. He'd learned emotions rather than macho from her. Interestingly, years later, Lily Tomlin, who worked with Travolta in *Moment by Moment* in 1979, said of her co-star: 'Maybe the major thing is how sensual he is. And how sexy too. Sensitivity and sexuality are very strong.

'It's as if he has every dichotomy – masculinity, femininity, refinement, crudity.'

Producer Lorne Michaels caught the same feeling from the 70s star Travolta: 'John is the perfect star for the 1970s. He has this strange androgynous quality, this all-pervasive sexuality. Men don't find this terribly threatening. And women, well…'

Women always loved Johnny Travolta. Ellen Travolta remembers her little brother as vacillating between aggressiveness and shyness: 'At eight Johnny would worry about the passing of time, and say to me: "Ellen, do you realise that we are never going to experience this moment ever again. It has already passed." He was a very heavy little boy.'

He was also a dreamer. He always wanted to be free, like a butterfly. Fame brought him the money to buy his own aeroplanes but at sixteen he was taking flying lessons at New Jersey's local Teterboro Airport. Four years later, in 1974, he was a licensed pilot of prop aircraft and six years later cleared for jets. For the rest of his life when he was confronted with difficult decisions or disappointments he would always take off, fly himself if possible, and get out of the town he was in. That way he seemed better able to adapt to and deal with what was facing him.

As a child he could only read about planes, and make plastic models with his father who would swing him around as his son screamed: 'Fly Daddy, Fly!' 'He was very, very curious,' recalled his father adding, 'He wanted to know the answer to everything like "How far up is the sky?" and "Why can't you make me an airplane that can fly?" Always aviation.

In 1996 he explained what he believes turned him into a sky-high junkie: 'The path of the airport was such that they went over New Jersey if they were going westbound (Hollywood, that is). They were about two thousand feet above the ground, struggling up, full loads, DC-6s, DC-7s. I'd have dreams about the people in them, people who were going places. It was a very romantic vision to me. I watched the jet age come through.'

The roaring silver birds always intrigued him: 'When Ellen started travelling I'd go with my parents to the airport to see her off. I was about five. In those days watching planes take off and land was a kind of entertainment. Families dressed up for the occasion including mine. It was a glamorous and wonderful ritual.

'I'll never forget my first plane trip. I flew with Ellen on National Airlines to Philadelphia. I had a grilled cheese sandwich and Coke and then flew back home. The first leg was on a four-engine propeller-driven airliner but we returned on a jet!

'I thought about being a professional pilot. I investigated all the possibilities but I didn't think I was enough of a scholar to do it, through the military or otherwise.'

Three decades later Travolta had put his passion for flying into a book. 'It's a homage to the great aviation experiences I had while growing up.' It is semi-autobiographical and tells about a boy's first flight across America. The manuscript entitled *Repeller One Way Nightcoach* sat in a desk drawer in 1996.

Travolta's other flights of fancy happened on an altogether different medium – the television. Annie Travolta, who in the late 1990s ran a travel agency in Los Angeles, remembers her brother 'going ape' over the television re-runs of *Yankee Doodle Dandy* with James Cagney in his 1942 Oscar-winning performance: 'Johnny loved it. He would dance in front of the television and do all of Cagney's steps. Johnny's whole childhood was filled with playing roles from small skits to acting in front of the TV. But of all of them his favourite was Cagney.'

And before the end of the century 'little Johnny' might play his idol ('I loved him, he was so loving and sensitive') in a biographical film being planned for the late 1990s of the legendary actor, the hoofer turned tough guy. Before he died Cagney told Travolta – and many others in Hollywood – that Travolta should play him in any authorized movie of Cagney's life.

Drag artist, dancer, stripper, singer, actor – toddler John Travolta was also a mimic and in his 40s he can impersonate almost everybody he has met – or a star like Joan Crawford from the television screen. He'll do it for you and even make it difficult. Raising his chin and flicking his wrist he says haughtily; 'Take a letter. Tell my fans I'm taking my shirt off.' It sounds like Joan Crawford but it's one better –

it's Faye Dunaway playing Joan Crawford in *Mommie Dearest*.

'My mother loved that Joan Crawford era. We were truly a theatrical family. My mother used to mirror those old movie star poses – the ones they used to do in magazines like *Photoplay*. We have pictures of her holding my sister Ellen up and kissing her in profile like the stars did in the magazines.'

Like mother, like son, his impersonations are boundless: Streisand, Cyndi Lauper, Stevie Wonder and even Warren Beatty. Travolta squints, 'You have to know Warren to appreciate it. Warren has a little trouble with his eyes that borders on Hasidic.'

Everyone and everything was always material for little Johnny. At the age of seven he decided to play Pa. His sister Annie recalled, 'He tried to smoke one of Dad's cigars. He had a big smile on his face. He looked so funny and he was taking Dad off great. But all of a sudden he turned green and he got sick. Real sick. I don't think he's ever smoked a cigar since except in acting roles.'

And he was always one for the ladies. Ten-year-old John Travolta would host spin-the-bottle parties (he got to kiss whoever the bottle was pointing to when it stopped). He thought he was suave like Sean Connery as 007 James Bond in *Dr No*. Ursula Andress, the first ever Bond girl, was – and remained – his perfect woman. 'My sexual ideal is your traditional well-built woman meaning large breasts, small waist, good hips, good butt, good legs,' he pronounced in the mid-1980s. But, according to his boyhood girlfriend Nancy Magdits, in and out of the school playground he was no short-pants Bond. 'I remember the first time Johnny kissed me. It was a really wet, horrible and sloppy kiss – I needed a towel! I said, "That's the wettest – ugh – kiss I've ever had." And Johnny just looked at me as if I was crazy and said, "Don't you like it?" '

He didn't like school. His classmates thought he was aloof. In fact, he was contemplative, a loner. His mother judged, 'He was a dreamer. He didn't do well simply because he wasn't paying attention.'

He was failing in three subjects at St Cecilia's Catholic Elementary School when he was moved to the Dwight Morrow High School on the outskirts of Englewood. 'He hung around the lockers and imitated the girls walking down the hall,' recalled his junior-high-school friend Aaron Wides. One of their classmates, Michelle Polak, remembers the games they got up to: 'John and I ended up a lot in the principal's office for our various pranks. John sat behind me in class and one day he twisted my hair in such a way that it looked like I had horns. I was so embarrassed.'

His imitations of Elvis, The Beatles and his teachers were his way of combating the antagonism of the playground bullies who resented his standoffish attitude. But some mimicry went too far. He and his classmate Larry Delaney were doing poorly in their language class and Larry said, 'We were both behind in our German homework. There was this girl in class who always got As on her homework so one day we took her homework and cut it up in four or five pieces and taped them on our papers. We were too lazy to even copy the answers over in our own handwriting. The teacher caught us and gave us a lecture.'

Travolta tried to fool his teachers with clever conversation or, as he puts it, 'I tried to communicate with them on a more adult level.' He was trying the same thing at home but his parents, especially his mother, didn't want to lose the family 'baby'. His determination to be grown-up, to be an adult, wasn't working at school or at home. It was a depressing time for him as 60s youth was rebelling and screaming for attention across America and the world, in New York and Chicago, in London, Paris and Rome. The world was growing up but he wasn't. Yet.

The early teens of John Travolta were filled with good and bad dreams and make-believe. He wasn't comfortable with himself or his surroundings. 'The kids at school thought I was a bit off because I was always rather odd. I wasn't really good-looking as a teenager. As a matter of fact, I was rather awkward looking. I felt my nose was too big for my face. I was very skinny – out of proportion. It took a time before I started growing into my looks. I didn't enjoy school and I really wasn't that good as a student. I was always cutting classes.

'I was more interested in anything *other* than what was going on in the classroom.'

Playing different parts was a release. He would pretend to be Jewish to get into the Englewood Jewish Community Centre, which was banned to gentiles. 'We used to get in by making up stories,' said Donald Di Lorenzo who played the charade with his schoolfriend. 'We'd give Jewish-sounding names at the door and say we came from some other temple. Johnny's brother Joey did the same thing. If that didn't work we would climb the walls and go in through the windows at the back of the building.'

The attraction of the Centre was the dances, at one of which Travolta met Denise Wurms. It was infatuation at first dance. 'I was fifteen and Johnny was fourteen. A friend introduced us,' remembers the dark-haired girl with the quick, wide grin. They 'dated' for nearly five years and Denise said: 'I found out right away that he was easy to talk with and our relationship was like apple pie. We were very close. He was my best friend.'

It was 1967/1968 and what Travolta calls 'my favourite teenage year'. 'I was discovering girls. And that was good. That was also the year I flew on airlines a lot. That made me happy. I found my first steady girlfriend in Denise. She looked like Ali MacGraw. She was kind of an earth girl, brunette. Tall girl, 5ft 8ins. I was 6ft by that time. She was the first girl that was brave enough to be, like, overtly crazy about me. I dug that. It was a great year. I had sought after girls that weren't responding to me the way I expected and this girl was responding to me exactly like I expected.

'She expressed it the way she danced with me to "Tighten Up" by Archie Bell and the Drells. She was a good dancer. It's kind of a rolling thing with your hands but then you put your foot out side to side, that's the tighten up.'

One squeeze led to another. 'It happened my favourite year – 1968. I guess I was 14. It was either her house or my house. We were in the middle of the sexual revolution – it wasn't that big a deal.'

But it kept them very close.

He says he did not have any religious qualms: 'It was more Irish guilt than Catholic. My father was very open about sex but my mother was more reserved. They really adored each other. My father thought my mother was the living end, that she was the best actress, the best director and had the most style, presence and personality of anyone he had ever known. They had a very hot relationship. Even after they'd been married for years you could walk into their bedroom in the morning – something I used to do as a kid – and there they'd be, nestled in each other's arms, their bodies totally locked together. They were really into each other.'

Later, Denise would visit him as he toured America in stage shows. She was his *girlfriend*, and when he was nineteen he almost married her. But, as it would be with almost all of his relationships, the friendship had been established long before any sexual liaisons. ('I only sleep with people I know and trust,' was John's 1980 view on sex and fidelity.) Denise was a soul sister. They grew up together and their relationship always had the quality of first love: close but not forever. In his fading school days, though John Travolta was a one-girl man. It allowed him the freedom to mix freely with *everyone* without having to make commitments.

The teenage Travolta found it easy being around girls. He was a charming clown while other boys were strutting their stuff, showing off. Travolta, even then, was, in *his* way, cool.

'Johnny always liked women a lot and felt more at ease around them than with the boys who were all into drinking and running about,' said Morse Place neighbour and classmate Eileen Fanning. 'Johnny was not like that. He would fool around to pass the time but he wasn't a wild one.'

His school days were something of a showbusiness education: wanting acceptance, getting rejection. Wanting to please, being misunderstood or ignored. But he learned something – more dance steps. Denise Wurms' brother Jerry, a tall, fair-haired, round-faced kid with the same instant smile as his sister, was his closest friend at school and would later work in Travolta's film production company. He remembers their teenage rock 'n' roll days: 'We were both taught to dance by the blacks. Somebody in the corridors or outside always had a radio and somebody was always dancing.'

Travolta remembered too: 'Whatever new dance came to school, I learned it. I think the blacks accepted me because I cared about them accepting me. They seemed to have a better sense of humour, a looser style. I wanted to be like that. All the qualities that made me remotely appealing to the masses are the black qualities I have as a person – my sense of humour, my dancing, my openness, sexually, with my movements. When I transferred to a public school that was predominantly black, right away I loved the black people. And they loved me because I could dance and was funny to them. The white kids never laughed at me, only the black kids. So it was the first time I was accepted by the masses. Like the blacks I simply called things as they were.

'I was always attracted to women with open sexuality and it was the same with blacks. I sensed their strong sexuality and it made me feel comfortable. They'd always say: "Hey, Travolta. Get your fine ass over here! You wanna fuck me?" It was always real open.

'And when you danced with a black girl you could grind and get down without necessarily meaning you were going to have sex with her. It simply meant you could move seductively and enjoy it. So I felt very safe with them, expressing myself verbally and physically. The first girl I ever kissed properly was a black girl. 'I was twelve and she was sixteen. She introduced me to reefer. She said: "Did you ever soul kiss?" And I said: "No, I don't think so." And she said: "Well, come over here and let me try it with you." So we kissed. I loved her because she was so complimentary; she thought I was fine and I thought she was fine too. I loved talking with my black friends about sex. They'd go into vivid descriptions without any shame at all. I loved it because it satisfied my voyeurism. Actually, I wish I could talk frankly about sex with white people as I do with blacks.

'See, I love talking about sex in detail – I like talking about what I like to look at, what I like to feel, what I like to experience but I always edit myself around white people.

'I could move my hips like other white boys couldn't when I was about five years old. We were all performers in our household! Our city was very successfully integrated – the music was very influential. I fell in love with The Beatles but my dance abilities were expressed through all of Motown. It was a sound to move to and feel. So, I lived a dual life.

'I was very aware of Elvis as a kid and his songs would play on the radio a lot. It was either Beach Boys' stuff or Elvis. But when The Beatles came in I fell in love like everybody else. 'I had a Beatle moptop. I did, I did! I was kicked out of school because of my Beatle haircut. The nuns grabbed it and said, "Cut it!"

'I have a theory – every man and woman represents a Beatle. You're either a Paul type, a George type, a Ringo type or a John type. John Travolta is Paul, baby. Paul all the way. Because I liked him so much when I was little. Who I wanted to be was Paul. Who I actually am other people can answer better.

'I have a special feeling for the whole *Sergeant Pepper* album. I felt there was something new happening and I went with it. I was 13 – I dropped out of school three years later – and the year of that album, 1967/1968 was my year. My favourite year back then.'

But the music and his dancing only eased the frustration. He talked to his parents about it but they, like all parents, saw his future in education and diplomas. His parents both understood his cravings, his restlessness. But they hoped it was a phase he would grow out of.

Travolta admitted later that he took advantage of being the youngest: 'None of my friends were allowed to eat as much candy as me.' It resulted in his lifelong love of calorie-packed goodies like hot fudge sundaes and tuna-melt sandwiches. And losing weight became more and more difficult. His freedom provoked a bitter rivalry with his brother Joey. 'I was a brat from age five to about fifteen. It was tough for everyone around me. I used to fight and get into scrapes. There were gangs in my neighbourhood and for a couple of years I was a mascot for one gang. But I grew out of that – just like I grew out of school.'

By his mid-teens he knew it was time to move on. By then the rather gangly, awkward out-of-it school loner had matured. He was confident, sure of himself. It showed. He was a performer.

One afternoon, driving back on the school bus from a football game some of the mostly black team began singing a James Brown number. It had the chorus:

Say it loud, I'm black and I'm proud.

Student John Travolta already knew that timing is everything and he waited his moment before chanting:

Say it light, I'm white and outasight!

Chapter Four
Infant Star

'Acting is a particularly fortunate profession. I am in a perpetual state of infancy'

Marcello Mastroianni, age 71, in 1996

The young John Travolta was taking his showbusiness career seriously. More than three decades later he considered that he had given himself over to acting when he was 13. He'd had his unofficial classes in ethnic rhythms and the paid-for ones at the Fred Kelly Dancing Academy but he wanted the star-making discipline he had been told about by his mother and witnessed on stage.

He knew he had the talent to make it. Tall with a lean frame and with the full lips, transparent blue eyes and the prominent nose that now matched the rest of his features, he was set to swagger and swing. ('When I was fifteen I would spend hours gazing at myself in front of the mirror.') He was sixteen when he left school and home. 'I decided I was good enough to compete with the professionals. So I went to New York City.'

Geographically, it wasn't a long trip, Mentally, for a youngster brought up with a cushioned, elaborate emotional safety net, it was a giant step. He would confront the single life, together with the hazards of sex and drugs both of which he would indulge in.

He admits that for a couple of years after he left home he could have self-destructed but a combination of ambition and belief in himself protected him. You sense, however, that most of all it was his determination to prove to his parents, his mother in particular, that he could succeed, that he could make his and their dreams come true, which kept his feet on the ground.

His confidence in his dancing and acting and singing had been building – 'all of it' he would yell to himself as he paraded around Englewood. But all along his mother had been there – in some cases literally – to hold his hand.

Although his family recall his *Gypsy* striptease and his Jimmy Cagney routines – he still does a great 'You dirty rat!' – John Travolta's memories start at around the age of twelve. He'd been onstage in his mother's productions; in one play his part was smaller than his brother Joey's and he protested with a tantrum, walking off stage.

In an interview shortly after he had become one of the world's leading stars with *Saturday Night Fever* he would reveal just how green he had been in the beginning about acting. Working with Ma was one thing but then there was the real thing. By happy coincidence the Actors' Studio of New York, stamping ground for some of America's giant acting names like Brando, De Niro and Pacino, staged teaching workshops in Englewood. Helen Travolta was in the front row with her aspiring thespian son.

'The first time I visited class I came in when some of the studio people, the advanced students from New York, were in the middle of doing a scene. After a couple of minutes they, like, broke character to ask the director a question and I was *stunned*. I mean, I didn't know they'd been *acting* – that's how believable they were!

'My mother got me in as an observer but she didn't have to urge me. Nobody pushed me into showbusiness. I was aching for it.'

It was a slow but positive – and lucky – beginning.

Lois Zetter, whose late partner Bob Le Mond first discovered John Travolta as a pimply, gawky fifteen-year-old, now lives in Las Vegas. She attended the ShoWest convention there in March 1996 when Travolta was honoured, and she remembered Le Mond's early impressions: 'What Bob saw in addition to talent was charisma. We always said there were three important qualities needed for acting. One is talent, one is a marketable look and one is charisma. 'If you have two out of three you'll be an actor. But you need all three to be a star. John had all three.'

Travolta immediately joined the Actors Studio and was cast as the juvenile lead in their production of *Who'll Save the Ploughboy?*. He had three lines. But that trio of attributes were evident, and when Travolta cast his mind back in later years he admitted, 'I could sort of duplicate what I saw these people do in class as soon as I saw it. I didn't mean to imitate them – I mean, I always did have the ability to observe people, watch them awhile, and very quickly absorb essence and then reproduce it. Nobody told me to do that.

'I just always stored things up about people and when I had a character to create I found I had this whole reserve of behaviour and mannerisms to draw on. You remember the guys you knew who are like the guy you are playing, you build a character that way. The last thing you do is add your own emotions to the script. That part's the most important of all. It's like inside a character's facade, *I* live. I really come alive when I'm doing that.'

Travolta's first break came when he landed a leading role as oddball loser Hugo Peabody in a New Jersey revival of the Broadway play *Bye Bye Birdie*. His mother was over the moon. She offered tips and called them 'notes', like professional theatre folk. The play is about loyalty and false idols but for the over-the-top-keen New

Jersey kid it meant money (fifty dollars a week) and, better still, applause. 'The first time I saw my name up on a billboard I felt it was really glamorous. But then I remembered the *Travolta Tire Exchange* sign my father had...'

'It was on one of those dinner theatre places out in New Jersey that Bob first saw John,' said Lois Zetter. 'You know, plastic chicken, a glass of wine and a show. Bob would be told of some act and go out to watch the shows because that was the breeding ground for young talent. John was clearly worth following-up. Bob didn't know his exact age and when John told him he was only fifteen he was surprised but he wanted to sign him up there and then. Bob liked to to think he was relaxed about it but he was excited at the prospect. Later when he told the story he would play it more low-key.

'He had some 'Le Mond – Zetter Agency' letterheads with him, contracts all ready to go. He put John on the spot and I think that was when – if there was ever an exact moment – John decided to go for it full time and drop out of school. That was a big decision – a big thing. There were was a lot of stigma about being a high school drop-out. Bob left his card and asked – no, insisted – that John call him. He did eventually.'

It took Travolta three and a half weeks to call Bob Le Mond. Even then he knew the value of waiting, of dangling someone before making a decision. It worked with girls and, seemingly, with acting. Le Mond was an actors' agent. He had started in New York and it was a daily grind. He aimed for dollars but was genuinely concerned about the well-being of his clients.

When Travoltamania whipped up a media hurricane in 1977, Le Mond told his version of their first meeting. A friend had gone on and on at him about this young guy out in some remote summer stock production of *Bye Bye Birdie*. 'Out in New Jersey, for Chrissakes!'

'I was dragged out there yelling and complaining,' recalled Le Mond: 'Well, my friend was right. I couldn't take my eyes off him. I went backstage to congratulate him and suggested he give me a call.'

When that call finally came Le Mond realised this particular talent needed special care and attention. He had watched what he believed was the exploitation of 1976 Olympic swimming champion Mark Spitz. He thought 'money-happy agents' and their 'million-dollar deals' had lost Spitz the best chance at cashing in on his seven gold medals. 'It was obvious in Spitz's case that the deal became the star. The guy wasn't ready. I didn't want that to happen to my kids. Timing is all important. You have to figure out what's suitable and when.'

Bob Le Mond always thought Hollywood was exceptionally suitable for Travolta. When? *Now*. It took just a little longer.

Travolta had all the professional and friendly support he could wish for from the man who was to make him a star and a millionaire. All he needed was the family version from his parents and that was never in question.

'We knew Johnny wasn't a bum and he knew he could count on us,' is how his mother remembered her baby's announcement that he wanted to go it alone. His father recalled, 'We never said to Johnny, "Why don't you become a priest like your cousin Frankie?" We never wanted him to be anything but what he wanted to be. It takes a long time for a kid to make it in showbusiness.'

Not John Travolta. In early 1996 he said of that first big step to stardom, 'My father wanted me to get my high school diploma and so he said, "Look, you go out and do your thing – if you don't do it in one year you agree to come back." By the end of that year I'd scored my Equity [actors' union] card and starred in summer theatre and had five commercials under my belt. My dad said, "What can I say? You did it." '

Time and memory tint the situation. His brothers and sisters recall it as a more traumatic period. There was something of a face-off between Helen and Sam Travolta and their youngest child who, all involved admitted at one time or another, was 'very spoiled'. His sister Margaret, in 1996 a housewife in Chicago, said, 'My father had built what was really a theatre in the basement. Complete with curtains – everything. Almost every night we would do musicals and our parents would be the audience. They were always praising us whether we were good or bad. It was interesting because you always felt there was a show going on in the house.

'It also meant there was a little bit of vying for attention. As the youngest, Johnny got more than his share of attention. He was my mother's youngest child and she knew she wasn't going to have any more. So, to her, this was a little blessing in disguise.

'We all kowtowed to Johnny pretty much. He was a little bratty but no more so than other kids.'

When his parents resisted his plans to leave school Travolta shifted from A to T, angst to tears. It was a worthy performance. When the trade-off was finally agreed in his favour there were hugs and promises, all of which were kept. Before he ever became a star he had learned the Italian lesson of family loyalty.

When he had been a youngster doing his basement shows, he said his parents 'would sit there from nine to midnight. They'd just be there. Always were.

'My father really didn't want me to quit school but my mother was really always on my side. She didn't want to take sides, you understand, but I always knew she was with me. Dad knew too. I wanted acting and singing and dancing, all of it. All of it. I always wanted all of it. Dad really didn't want me to quit. My mother said to him, "He's sixteen and should be able to make his own choice." That was when the deal was made.

'My mother was outwardly emotional and I was the kind of kid who liked to play on people's emotions. I had always threatened her with things, frightening things like if I didn't get to fly to Chicago to see my sister I'd jump out of the window. Seeing her react strongly was fascinating to me.'

And Helen Travolta was someone, according to a family friend, who ' would kill for her Johnny'. Her son sees it as funny now but it must have been quite a scene, the two 'stars' of the family wanting the stage and wanting their way. He said, 'When I was six years old I said to my mother that if she didn't make me chocolate pudding I'd cut off my weenie. She made the pudding – fortunately.'

Even in his 40s Travolta would describe some anatomical matters and intimate functions with words from childhood. Over a big business lunch/interview in the Polo Lounge of the lavish Beverly Hills Hotel with a glossy American man's magazine in 1995 he excused himself from the table, telling the surprised writer,'I've got to go pee-pee.' Once, a lifetime earlier, while wandering near his house he saw a neighbour with his pregnant wife. Travolta gushed at him, 'Oh, you must have a high sperm count.' It was awkward humour that provoked an awkward moment. But Travolta laughed at his one-liner and bounced away.

However crass such remarks, they were always well intentioned. But it got him a reputation for being dumb. At 16 he felt guilty that it looked as though he would be the only one in the family not to graduate from high school but he felt he had no choice but to take his chance: 'I had no shot at proper schooling. I had no patience. It was like, give it a shot. One hundred percent. Or start handling luggage at the airport.'

He had his parents' blessing which was vitally important. He didn't need even the weeniest bit of blackmail and when the fame had come, gone and come back again he said, 'My parents were rooting for me all along. That's why I respond to people like Quentin [Tarantino] because they remind me of my mother and father. I'm attracted to people who have that kind of love for me and let me know. I flourish under that kind of passion and I don't do well without it.'

Bob Le Mond, a quietly spoken man with sharp features, a neatly trimmed beard and receding, dark hair, was managing the client he had so desperately wanted.

'I don't think Bob ever doubted that John would get in touch,' said Lois Zetter.' And Bob wanted John on stage or on film. He was a good-looking boy and the way to go was commercials.'

Bob Le Mond would tell everyone about his discovery, and said later, 'He got the first part I sent him up for. He was a dream, he never got turned down for anything I sent him up for in those early days.'

Travolta's film debut was in a 1974 television advertisement selling life insurance for the Mutual of New York company. There was a video-taped screen test and Irving Johns, the ad's creative director, said, 'He looked at the cameras, delivered his lines, and the hair on the back of your neck stood up.'

It was a short role but he had been made for it. In a leather jacket his character strides down a street in New York's Staten Island towards the camera. He talks straight to camera about his father, who cared for and planned everything. Everything except his death.

It was a hit, and then he was in Hagar slacks or driving a Honda – he did about forty upscale commercials. The Le Mond – Zetter Agency payslips for that time show his progress: he received $220 for that first Mutual of New York screen test and then $2,500 for the completed commercial. The next time around, when he had become a prime time television star he got $20,000. Later, when he was an Oscar nominee, there wasn't enough money.

But Bob Le Mond wasn't being smug. The commercials were for eating-and-audition money. There were a couple of small, out-of-state gigs and some summer stock near Pittsburgh in next-door Pennsylvania. His client was still staying at home but more and more he yearned to have his own place. Drugs played their part in his urge to move out from Morse Place. His image has always been as an in-control, drug-free star who rarely drinks more than a couple of glasses of wine with meals. That was and is the established John Travolta. But he revealed that as a teenager he was not immune to temptation from the 'in' crowd:

'I don't use drugs but from sixteen to eighteen I did marijuana. It always made me sick – physically ill. Then, when I was eighteen or nineteen I had trouble sleeping and I took some Seconals but that was short-lived.

'I tried cocaine too when I was about seventeen but it didn't take either. I know that I have this image of being anti-drugs and I am if it hurts you, but really I don't care what other people do. It is none of my business. The reason I don't do drugs is because I don't have a good physical reaction to them. It's the same with drinking.'

As Bob Le Mond knew, for once in the starmaking business he had a headliner whom success was not going to spill over the top. 'He had the great advantage over the stars of the past, the Marilyn Monroes, the Monty Clifts, and that was that he wasn't neurotic or self-destructive.'

But his client was sensitive in later years about his 'overnight' success. 'The luck came fast but not success, OK?' he said touchily to an early interviewer. He would repeat: 'I was not an instantaneous success.'

Later, he remembered, 'I moved into New York, into this condemned building at 56th Street and Eighth Avenue. A bunch of actors lived there – my sister Annie, myself, our friends. The elevator was a death-trap, the heating didn't work. But that's fun when you're a teenager. New York was a big playground, man!'

With the help and attention of Bob Le Mond Travolta was soon a repertory regular on the New York stage. The only place it was chilly was inside that dilapidated apartment at 56th and Eighth. But, hell, he was hot in New Yawk.

The picture, then, is of an eager-to-please young lad who without any doubt had talent. He could sing and dance and act. He had a personality for every corner of New York's Lower West Side.

In Englewood he had undergone seven months of psychoanalysis and explained, 'My friends didn't really understand me – they thought I was a bit off because I was interested in theatre. How could I share my kind of experience? I'd have such pain I'd be crying.'

This kind of thinking recurred – in his dark moments when he wasn't 'on' – in New York. He had the longtime romantic notion, that suffering for *Art* is the surest way to artistic purity. And the fastest. He picked his friends carefully, for their misery, their down moods.

'I was very impressionable at the time. I was proud of my neurosis. There was a Peter Allen song, "Back Doors Crying", that seemed to sum up what the period was like:

"Thought I was happy only when I was sad.
Let go of good things, hung on to the bad."

'It was like whoever's darker or more neurotic was the more talented. What the fuck does that mean? I decided to drop it all and started to do well.'

He never lost his concerns, even with success and the trappings that came with it. Bob Le Mond would point out later, 'He worries about every take in a movie. He worries whether the avocados are going to get ripe on his trees. It comes from being a perfectionist. But his sensitivity and vulnerability are exactly what made him a star.'

Travolta disagreed. He thought, 'I have a fortunate thing. I can think a thought and it comes through. I don't know whether it's my light eyes or presence or what, but I have to do very little.

'I have an actor's face. I can be handsome, ugly, romantic, nasty, all according to the camera's angle.'

The camera loved him. Full frame. Centre stage. So, luckily, did America and then the world. He was on his way to become the first male movie star of his generation. Redford, Newman, Eastwood, Nicholson, even newcomers like Stallone and Nick Nolte from television's first mini-series *Rich Man, Poor Man*, were older. Then, as in the 1990s, moviegoers aged fifteen to twenty-four made the stars and, in reverse, dictated the movies the stars made for them.

Travolta was speeding towards icon status as a figure-head for late 70s youth. Looking at it another way, he was a kid with a passion for acting and flying – Howard Hughes loved the same things – who was trying to cope with that often mind-numbing rush of wealth and celebrity and the attendant 'Yes' brigade. And, of course, giant circuses of clowns.

'He had a vision of where he wanted to be,' said director Tom Moore. 'I have a crazy theory. I think John created a vacuum and then stepped into it. He *willed* his success.'

But could it last?

Patricia Birch, as the choreographer of the stage and Hollywood versions of *Grease,* helped make Travolta a worldwide star. She was a close friend to the young actor-dancer and believed he had 'the guts to be there all the way'. But she says there was always some doubt beneath the bravado: 'He always thought it could be a fleeting, sex-symbol thing. And, oh goodness me, he didn't want that.

'John had his heart in this for life…'

Chapter Five
Hello, Marilu

'He and I were never ones to miss our cue for passion.' Marilu Henner on her

backstage sexploits with John Travolta

Auditions, auditions, auditions. The theatre meat market. It was a daily run-around searching for the big one. 'Those who wait, wait tables,' was John Travolta's explanation to his wannabe-star buddies about his aggressive hunt for decent roles.

Fuelled by his own ambition and accelerated by Bob Le Mond's guidance, the young career tearaway found himself in blink-and-you-won't-see-me roles in the daytime television soaps. They were good rehearsals. He had time for everything, commercials, soaps, shows. If he didn't win the role he went up for he would usually be found something. He was an engaging lad and his personality won through in a world of engaging lads.

It was when he was appearing in a small production of Somerset Maugham's *Rain* that he met actress Joan Prather and heard for the first time about Scientology. They liked each other, shared the same goals and dreams. She was four years older and they would talk backstage about the chances of bigger shows, better roles. There were evenings when he was low and one in particular when he had heard that he had lost the chance for the lead role in Dominick Dunne's film *Panic In Needle Park*. Dunne was seeking a dark Italian-type for his movie about junkie life in New York. Another, older actor was up for the role, but Robert De Niro didn't get the lead either. It was that other worthy candidate, Al Pacino, who made it his film debut.

Travolta, of course, had no frame of reference then to know or understand the future Oscar-winning talents with whom he had been in competition. But, like someone dealing positively with their first car crash, he climbed out of his wrecked hopes and got straight back in the driving seat. But, he told Joan Prather, he felt down.

And the downs could get very low and not just because of lost roles: sometimes he just felt *low*. He told her that analysis had not done much good. He didn't want other people's help. He wanted to help himself. Joan Prather told him about Scientology – it was very much an overview because she'd learned it took time to present everything about the religion – and Travolta was interested. It sounded like something for him.

At eighteen he was already dealing with some grown-up hang-ups. But work came first. And it presented itself at rehearsals for the national touring group for *Grease*. The show was to play across America and work was beginning at the Ansonia Hotel at Broadway and West 73rd Street in New York. All the big stage names, even the ballet and opera guys, had got their acts together at the Ansonia's rehearsal hall.

His sister Annie had won an understudy contract for the tour and Travolta danced right in too. An actress (with what cast member Jerry Zaks loudly described as 'sensational tits') called Marilu Henner, just two years older than Travolta, waltzed in alongside. Everybody noticed her. She was voluptuous.

She and Travolta were the youngest in the cast. As Henner explained in her 1993 autobiography, *By All Means Keep on Moving*, she had much in common with her new co-star: both were from Catholic families; both had two brothers and three sisters; his mother taught theatre, hers taught dance; his father sold tyres, her father sold cars; they were both from homes that were neighbourhood HQs.

The 'youngsters', as they were known to the rest of the cast, were both earning more than $300 a week. They were also doing what they wanted – well, getting close. Travolta was playing mild-mannered Doody of the Jets while Henner was one of the Pink Ladies. Judy Kaye was the lead lady Rizzo, and Jeff Conway, who would later be Henner's co-star in the huge television success *Taxi*, had the role of Danny Zuko that Travolta craved.

Rehearsals, rehearsals, rehearsals, had replaced the audition regimen. Away from the Ansonia, Travolta, Henner and Ellen March, who played Frenchie, would go to see 50s movies in the name of research: they saw James Dean in *Rebel Without A Cause* and Brando in *The Wild One*. 'What are you rebelling against?', Henner would dead-pan to Travolta who would return Brando's 'Whatta you got?' They'd play spies and romantics, Astaire and Rogers.

This was fun. There were pranks on stage – a half-eaten lobster replaced a tuna sandwich during one performance and in another, to the audience's delight, Travolta used an oversized Disneyland comb to slick back his hair. In one scene Henner had to flip open her wallet and study a snapshot before singing 'Freddy I Love You'. Sometimes the photograph didn't show 'Freddy' but a nude man aimed at sending Henner into hysterics. But, like all the cast, she was a professional.

Travolta was learning a great deal. The contract for the *Grease* tour was thirteen cities in twelve months. It was slower than a Greyhound Bus but you got to meet show people. Throughout much of the tour Travolta shared a room with Michael Lembeck, whose father, Harvey Lembeck, was a veteran of movies like *Stalag 17* and the classic television series *You'll Never Get Rich* working with Phil Silvers as that other Travolta hero Sergeant Bilko.

'John loved to goof around. We'd all become so bored with the show that we began to play pranks,' Lembeck remembers.

'But the funniest ones were the things that John did. There we were as two tough gangs who are set to rumble. We were supposed to have a gang fight and our leader was supposed to pull a chain out of a trash can full of weapons on stage. John had put a teddy bear in there. So the tough gang leader reached into the trash can for his chains and when he pulled out his hand he was holding a teddy bear. We laughed so hard we could hardly finish the scene. Another time one of the guys was supposed to reach in his bag for a sandwich and he pulled out a wriggling crab – that was John too.

'I think his fun got him the role in the first place. He was trying out for spaced-out Doody. When he came on for his audition he deliberately walked into the piano. It was hysterical. The writers and producers fell out of their chairs. John got the part.'

Despite the pranks Henner believed then that Travolta, who was getting strong reviews, would be a big star. Women especially loved his character, whom Henner dubbed a 'vulnerable puppy-dog.'

Off-stage he was also vulnerable. He was seeking the elusive answer – the answer to life when he visited a gypsy fortune teller in Philadelphia. She gave charlatans a bad name. 'You live in a house, you come from a woman, you are a male.' Well, that was fine but then she warned, 'You have a terrible curse on your head. You have bad spirits all around. I get rid of the curse if you bring me linguine, tomato paste and Parmesan cheese.'

As far as Travolta knows the gypsy bought her own pasta dinner that night, but the incident cheered him up. What was there to be concerned about? He had a job, he was earning. And he had his girl at home, Denise Wurms.

He and Henner would sometimes fly off to Los Angeles when theatres they were playing went 'dark' on Sunday and Monday evenings. But it was a platonic relationship. They'd sleep in the same room, sometimes in the same bed but they were friends not lovers. They talked a lot about sex. Travolta liked talking, liked going into details. He talked about Denise, and Henner about her relationships. If she went to visit her family she'd bring back Travolta's favourite Uno's pizza for him.

Other people could see the 'couple' of John Travolta and Marilu Henner. Henner's sister JoAnn asked her, 'God, why aren't you madly in love with this guy?'

They were buddies, was the reply to all who asked.

But Travolta's relationship with his school sweetheart Denise was falling apart. Their lives had diverged and wilted through separation. Jerry Wurms was living in an apartment in Los Angeles and his sister was also out in California. By the time the *Grease* touring show reached the West Coast it was clear that the romance that could have resulted in a pre-fame marriage wasn't going to happen. Michael Lembeck explained, 'They were growing apart rather than together'. 'Finally, it was Denise who ended it. John wasn't prepared for that so it came as a shock to him. But it was – and he knew it – inevitable.'

Marilu Henner was renting an apartment in Westwood, the university district of Los Angeles, while Travolta was on Larrabee, which cuts steeply downhill from Sunset Boulevard to Santa Monica Boulevard – an area which later years became the gay centre of West Hollywood. It was very much a 'happening' area and time: restaurants and cafés bubbled with customers.

Travolta and Henner would go out to dinner most nights and talk, talk, talk until either the coffee or the conversation dried up. Usually it was the coffee supply that ended first. They had been on many away-trips together and planned one up the coast in San Francisco. In her autobiography, Henner recounts a visit to Disneyland. Travolta stopped her 'somewhere between Fantasyland and Adventureland' and said, 'You know, Henner, when we get up north this weekend, what do you think about *it* ?'

The Travelodge hotel at Golden Gate Bridge was where 'it' happened. Henner wrote, 'It was absolutely incredible, tender, open, passionate. It wasn't some big now-it's-the-time-for-me-to-seduce-you thing. Our slide into intimacy didn't have a dramatic movie score montage feel to it. But it was hardly disappointing. It was natural and effortless, more like: Oh, we're going to sleep over like we used to but now we get to play doctor too. There was a comfortable, exploratory feel to it and I felt closer to him than I ever had before.'

One way or another it was going to last. Travolta had waited until he was sure. He was still waiting for his movie break. He had scored some small roles in episodic television series like *The Rookies*, *Owen Marshall M.D.* and *Emergency* but was also auditioning for films. At the same time he was doing *Grease* at the Schubert Theatre, the 'stars' stage', in Los Angeles. And making love to Marilu Henner at every opportunity.

'He and I were never ones to miss our cue for passion,' she said. In her book she tells of their desperate need for each other. 'One hot rendezvous spot was a tiny first-aid room backstage at the Schubert. It was just down the hall from where the musicians entered the orchestra pit and had a cot and a lock. That was all we needed for the fifteen or twenty minutes between the first and second acts. To some such obstacles would have meant "Intermission Impossible". Not us. We decided to accept our mission. We did this more than a dozen times that summer and somehow never got caught.'

She says they played it out as a sexual fantasy. They pretended they were being kept after school for being bad and behaving even more badly in the nurse's room. She called it 'the ultimate detention fantasy'.

Travolta's dreams of becoming a star were becoming reality. He had been seen by several Hollywood players in *Grease* which throughout its run was a hot ticket in town. Behind the scenes Bob Le Mond was working contacts. The television slots increased. Travolta could do them *and* the show.

There were also movie calls and one was for *The Last Detail* which had potential. The director was the soaringly talented Hal Ashby and the lead Jack Nicholson. Like all good plots it was simple: a young sailor is on his way to jail but his escorts give the rather soft-headed lad a final touch of the outside, wine, women and song. It was a star-making role for the sailor pitched into the last-chance saloon and a landmark film for Nicholson. Travolta set his hopes on it.

He was in San Francisco with Marilu Henner when he checked in with Bob Le Mond only to discover that Randy Quaid, older brother of Dennis, had won the showcase role.

Travolta's reaction was to get on a plane. He and Henner took the Pacific Southwest Airlines (the 1970s pink hot-pants airline) shuttle flight from the Bay Area to Las Vegas. Taking to the skies became a running metaphor for the highs and lows of his career. Any bitterness was only hinted at later in something of a backhanded compliment he made to Quaid: 'Although it was a great role Quaid physically looked the part. He WAS that guy. I would have had to act out the role but I'm sure I could have done just as well.'

He and Marilu Henner shared *everything* now. She had never felt more alive. In love. Being loved. She couldn't stop talking about it. Even five years later when she was co-starring in *Taxi* she would recall their first times together: 'He was so eager to please'. She'd tell how he fed her and combed her hair after she broke a knuckle on her right hand. To hear her tell it, this was one devoted lover. But youthful passion could only disguise not hide the emotional joins. Travolta's life was still career led. He'd had a taste of Hollywood and he was getting addicted to it.

As well as wanting his own way.

Chapter Six
The Road to Durango

'I didn't mind the scene stealing.' Patty Andrews about co-star John Travolta

Many men were interested in Marilu Henner. She was fun and sexy, full of life and happy to enjoy it. Her main man continued to be Travolta but he was often away, mostly in Los Angeles, on auditions and their relationship, as it would be for many, many years, became 'open'. Although some months they talked more often on the telephone than in person they had made a pact 'never to desert each other'. They dated others but there were sparks and 'great sex' when they reunited. Although she knew he loved her, she also knew that his career came first. Certainly in those days of flirting with fame 'Mari, I love you,' took very much second place to 'Bob, what have you got for me?'

In later years Travolta would get irritated about what he thought was the greatest misconception about him, that he was insecure and uncertain from the beginning. 'I think people misinterpret my sensitivity or perceptiveness as insecurity and indecisiveness. I'm given less credit for being a strong individual than I deserve. I am strong.'

Analysts regard Travolta as a classic case perfectionist. He wants everything right – love, work, life. It's a tricky trinity to pull off. But that is the way he is.

Dr Jamie Turndurf, a psychoanalyst and New York radio-show host, said Travolta's youngest-child background made him 'want to prove himself to all the family. To show his parents and his siblings that he wasn't an afterthought. And it also makes people in his circumstances, talented people who are on a pedestal, want to be perfect. They don't want to allow others to be able to pick holes, find faults in their lives – their professional or their private lives. In extreme cases they want perfect people around them, perfect wife, perfect child – a perfect world.'

It sounds like a heavy burden to live up to but it's not too difficult to shrug off if you have the drive and confidence of a John Travolta. This was no naive young lad. He knew what he wanted. And that was Hollywood.

But he was always clever enough to listen to Bob Le Mond, the man whose mantra was 'timing is everything'. Travolta had more boards to pound. This time it was the Broadway stage with *Grease*. The show's director Tom Moore had become a good friend of Travolta and Marilu Henner. They had both proved themselves to him and he had no difficulty taking Travolta to Broadway.

By now Travolta knew the routine, he could do Doody upside down all over Manhattan, but he was totally dedicated. If he didn't hit his mark at a particular performance he would sulk at himself. He felt the spotlight was always on him: full voltage. If it wasn't he usually wanted to know why.

During his run with *Grease* he regularly took off for Los Angeles to try out for television roles. One break was an episode of *Medical Centre*, a popular hospital drama series (it ran from 1969 to 1975) which starred the toothsome Chad Everett of whom Travolta had been a boyhood fan.

Director Tom Moore was also developing *Over Here* a lavish musical presentation that would showcase the Andrews Sisters. The close-harmony singing group had been favourites on stage and in movies throughout the 1940s and they were to work with a young cast including dancer Ann Reinking and a hotly tipped actor called Treat Williams. Also in the cast of the big-budget Broadway musical were John Travolta and Marilu Henner. She was playing a waitress in love with black and white films, and Travolta, a soldier off to war, had a big finale number. During rehearsals before an out-of-town try-out in Philadelphia they stayed with his parents in Englewood and took the bus into the city every day. This seemed as good as it could be. They were together and they would laugh all the way to work 'running' their lines as they went.

In Philadelphia the perfection-seeking Travolta was hurled a curve. He had heard that Bette Midler (then a tremendous camp favourite in New York) was out in the audience and, of course, that was the performance when the elaborate backstage mechanics failed. The audience hardly noticed but he took umbrage. He was quitting, going to Los Angeles that night.

He was so down on himself and the show that he took himself off to Philadelphia airport. The only problem was he didn't have money for a bus ride, never mind an American Airlines flight to the west coast. Circumstances and Marilu Henner convinced him to stay with *Over Here* and he was there on 6 March 1974, opening night on Broadway. He took full advantage of his opportunity.

Patricia Birch, the choreographer on that show and an early fan, recalls, 'In *Over Here*, John was – what? – nineteen? Well, he was already very magnetic but that boy worked like a dray horse! His whole life was work. He's very attractive and he knew it; he had a fantastic sense of his own physicality and knew how to use it.'

He left no doubt about his ambition to Patty, the youngest of the Andrews

Sisters. She said she knew he was going to be a major name – he kept upstaging her. 'He wouldn't do it purposely. He was just so intent on his part. He was very creative and tried to make his part outstanding. He'd make something out of nothing.

'For example he'd do little schticks that weren't anywhere in the script and a few times he went right in front of me. Or when I would be doing an exit he would suddenly walk in front of me or something. I didn't mind the scene stealing. John was very ambitious without being aggressive. And he was a very sweet person.

'He would ask me different things about my career and I would give him advice, telling him to create and keep doing things better. He had a natural talent you can't teach anybody, and he knew he had it. He took his work seriously. He kept improving his part until he left the show. Everybody was kinda shocked – it was right in the middle of a successful Broadway run. I don't think he had any job waiting for him. He just wanted to get into television.'

So, of course, did Bob Le Mond. It was September1974, when Travolta left *Over Here* and by then he was free of personal attachments. He and Marilu Henner had shared an apartment for eight weeks in New York but had decided to get their own places. They both wanted to see other people, they said. Others say he was more intent on his career than anything else.

Maybe Travolta didn't realise what he had. He was confident about his talent, and about love, as though he would always have it. He would say later, 'I was very much loved by my family and when you're very much loved it takes a lot to convince you that you will not be loved. If someone didn't love me I would never equate it to mean that everyone doesn't love me.'

His reputation was good in New York and he was offered a strong role in a play that was to become a classy success, *The Ritz*, which starred established performers Rita Moreno and the late Jack Weston. But Chad Everett had a television series...Hollywood was fun. The apartments on Larrabee, Sunset Strip...The movies.

Even a salary in excess of $750 a week couldn't compete with the magical magnet of that HOLLYWOOD sign, which lures hundreds of hopefuls every year to try their Tinseltown luck. As far as John Travolta was concerned luck had nothing to do with it. Hard work was all. But you have to believe in happenstance. Especially in the movies.

Hollywood is a stretch from Broadway, and in Los Angeles Travolta was just another good-looking guy with an Equity card anxious to make it in television or, better still, in the movies. Desperate to jump ahead, he became more and more depressed and disappointed in himself for 'choosing negative people to be around'. Where was the feel-good factor?

Maybe the answer was in Mexico.

With *The Ritz* rejected before you could shout, 'Action!' he was up to his eyes in a daft monk outfit in his first feature film. It was called *The Devil's Rain* and filmed in Durango, a dusty town that John Wayne had put on the map with a string of Westerns including *The Sons of Katie Elder*. It's a bumpy ride down out of Guadalajara – and the pilots are always keen to get there for dinner as it's the last trip of the day. He shared his flight with a gaggle of locals with endless hand luggage and constant squeals of conversation. First, from the air, he saw the cowboy 'Dodge City' the movie people had constructed a decade earlier and it was more impressive than reality. Over the years many stars – including Wayne – had taken refuge in Tequila, for Durango, the bullseye of Mexico, offers little but heat and dust albeit with warm hospitality.

It was a low-budget horror picture but he could not complain about the cast: veteran tough guy and Oscar winner (1955's Best Actor for *Marty*) Ernest Borgnine and Ida Lupino (Miss Lupino to Travolta), who had not only worked with a gallery of Hollywood names but had become one of the industry's first female directors with *Not Wanted* in 1949. She had worked with Humphrey Bogart, George Raft and Edward G. Robinson – she knew Cagney!

Even better, Travolta met up again with dark-haired, happy-faced Joan Prather. The actress, who later established herself on ABC TV's *Eight Is Enough* family series, literally stood in for Marilu Henner and they became a couple.

The Devil's Rain was a very important movie for Travolta. It was after it that he was to devote himself – apart from one period of disillusionment – to Scientology. Joan Prather said, 'I had taken all my Scientology materials and books to Durango with me because I thought I'd have a lot of free time.

'Johnny was as depressed as I was. We were the only two young people there. It was a very lonely time for him. His friends were using him as a door wipe.

'One day Johnny got very ill with the flu. In Scientology, we do a thing called a "touch assist" which makes you get better much faster. It's not magic. If you have a broken bone it will heal in two weeks instead of six.

'So, I was giving him this "assist " and in the middle of it he looked around at me and said, "This is the first time anybody's ever really helped me without wanting anything back from it." I started showing him my Scientology books and he just couldn't read enough of them.'

Travolta remembers the moment in even more detail – twenty-one years later. 'It was January of 1975, which was eight months before I did the pilot for *Welcome Back, Kotter*. I remember it quite specifically because it was the biggest change in my life. It was something that really looked like it held a clue to what was going on.

'I had a cold and Joan Prather gave me what's called an assist, you know, touching and talking. You address the whole body but you go to the areas that are most bothersome. It really helped me. And then I had a sore throat and she did another process on me and the sore throat went away. So then I knew something's really working here. I said, "I need to find out more about this".'

Not Damascus then, but the Road to Durango.

Marilu Henner says she saw a change in Travolta after Mexico. 'He said Scientology made a tremendous difference to him and we talked a lot about it, but it wasn't for me.'

On these visits to New York following *The Devil's Rain* – his lines included shouting, 'Blasphemer, blasphemer' and his big moment, a special-effects vanishing trick, was to evaporate in a puddle of green goo – his meetings with Henner were purely platonic. He was seeing Joan Prather, although she insists, 'We were together for three months although I wouldn't call it dating. We were the best of friends. I'm very stable and I could see that he also wanted to be that way.'

Well, he wanted career stability. And the young Travolta fervently believed that from there everything else would lead. He got what he wanted. He survived the Mexican desert.

Now it was to be rumbles in the Hollywood jungle.

Chapter Seven
Welcome?

'I had a whole career in theatre before I became famous.' John Travolta, 1996

*T*he Devil's Rain* had not turned out to be a Savoy-style alternative to *The Ritz* but Bob Le Mond's chief client had a feature-movie credit. And a production company had sent over the script for the television pilot of an ABC TV show called *Welcome Back, Kotter*.

It had its roots in the British television series *Please, Sir*, which had been a vehicle for actor John Alderton. The American version had Gabe Kaplan who created it in the lead and who discovered, as to some degree Alderton had, that the 'class' wanted to be stars too. Unlike other British series, like *Porridge* and *Fawlty Towers* which were bought but bungled or a US adaptation of *Absolutely Fabulous* which was critically changed (drugs, cigarettes and Bollinger champagne by the gallon ruled unsuitable for American prime time television fare) or subdued like *Men Behaving Badly* (which they weren't after crossing the Atlantic), the US take on the mob from *Please Sir* worked.

Kaplan as Kotter returns to his own New York high school to teach the toughest kids, the 'Sweathogs'. The centre of attraction is Vinnie Barbarino, a good-looking Italian kid, shaggy-haired, head-to-toe narcissistic, who seems in control but underneath the leather jacket and crumpled T-shirt is a bumbling mess of hormones and insecurities.

On ABC TV then the big youth show was *Happy Days* starring Ron Howard – later to become the awarding-winning director of movies like *Apollo 13* and *Ransom*. Howard and others in the cast, including established character actors Marion Ross and Tom Bosley, had found themselves being edged out of the action by a young actor called Henry Winkler and his creation 'Fonzie', a.k.a. 'The Fonz'. He was a clever, leather-jacketed, narcissistic lady-killer. He was also in for some competition – on his own television network.

In an entertainment small world where *Kojak* breeds *Kolchak* and *Khan*, imitation is the greatest indication of ratings success. In the autumn of 1975 the cool crown was up for grabs.

'I felt it would go. Vinnie was a star-making role,' said Bob Le Mond, at his prophetic best. The series executive producer James Komack says he knew he had found his charismatic dumb-bell Vinnie Barbarino right away. It was casting at first sight. 'I had seen five or six guys but the moment I saw John I knew he was it. But I couldn't convince him he had the part. He refused to believe. He even followed me to New York where I had gone to cast the other roles, pestering me to test him for Barbarino. I told him he was crazy. He had nothing to gain and that a bad test could wind up costing him the part. He insisted. Fortunately for all of us he tested great.'

Komack trusted his instincts all the way. Later, however, Travolta's doubts could be better understood. Randy Quaid had 'stolen' his role in *The Last Detail* because, Travolta believed, he looked the part. He thought it would be that way again. 'I never thought I would get *Kotter*. It was never a sure thing. I was *sure* they'd say, "You could *act* the part but there's this other guy who *is* the part". ' Hindsight boosted his confidence. 'Mostly, they cast that way, but this time they went for the acting, which I really respected.'

Respect also brought $1,500 a week and money in the bank. When he had his first $5,000 he paid half of it (careful with money already) for a single-engine Aircoupe. Vinnie Barbarino wasn't going to make him break the sound barrier – but he got Travolta up in the sky, flying high.

Komack had surrounded Gabe Kaplan with strong players: Travolta, Ron Palillo as Arnold Horshack, Robert Hegyes as Juan Epstein and Lawrence Hilton Jacobs as 'Boom-Boom' Washington. Every one of them wanted action. Travolta most of all. Komack reflected:

'He helped shape Barbarino a great deal. Originally, Vinnie was very slick and very tough. He was a bully and a con artist. But Johnny has a very likeable, sweet and even soulful personality. He has a very spiritual attitude so we made Barbarino a devout Catholic. Because Johnny could play against Barbarino's conceits he made him an extremely vulnerable character.

'All four kids on *Kotter* were damn good. It fascinated me but didn't necessarily surprise me that John took off fastest,' added Komack, who was inadvertently responsible for another tangent of Travolta's career and something that would also change his life for ever. Komack blocked his star's first big movie break. With hindsight it is possible that he was trying to protect him as well as *Kotter*.

In an interview to America's *TV Guide* at the height of his show's success, Komack said, 'He's a brilliant actor. He's doing a great job for us. I just worry about his ambition. It's massive. He knows he's good and he knows he's hot. There's a danger, as a result, of his going the way of a David Cassidy and The Partridge Family and The Monkees, of hitting it big and then fading fast. Barbarino is only a small part of his total range. Frankly – and I speak as a former Broadway actor – I'm in awe of his talent. But I think that he's worried that his big chance will slip away.'

Because of his contract and filming schedules Travolta was unable to take the lead in Terence Malick's *Days of Heaven*, which was a turn-of-the-century *Easy Rider* (Richard Gere took the role). Komack said, 'I know he got upset with me for a while because he thought it was my fault he couldn't do the Malick film. I honestly tried to rearrange our shooting schedule to allow it but we simply couldn't pull it off.'

There were some choice rows. Komack still backs his corner claiming circumstances beyond his control but later added:

'He thought the movie would make him the next Jack Nicholson. And who knows? Maybe it could have. God knows, he had that potential. But I finally said to him, "Do you really want to be Nicholson now? After all, you'd still have to do *Welcome Back, Kotter*. Do you honestly see Jack Nicholson playing a supporting role in *Welcome Back, Kotter*? '

The question by then was whether Travolta could see himself playing a supporting role in a middle-of-the-road chancer of a situation comedy. It was just another pilot hoping for a ride on a network rainbow to the multi-million-dollar pot of gold that awaits a long running series with re-run potential.

Barbara Zuaniuch was a television writer for the now defunct Los Angeles *Herald Examiner* when *Kotter* made waves on the air. The show helped its network regularly beat CBS TV in the ratings and that meant hundreds of thousands of dollars in advertising revenue. Zuaniuch said that after only four months it was clear that Vinnie Barbarino – despite only half a dozen minutes of screen time in some episodes – was the star. She had lunch with him in January 1976.

'Travolta knew – he was already planning his spin-off series *Vinnie*. That's how sure of himself he was. After only a matter of weeks, which is no time at all in television. Four years maybe – but not four months.'

Pre-publicity had helped *Kotter*. It had been banned in Boston and a string of other conservative places. City authorities believed that the antics of a classroom of rowdies might incite similar activities throughout America's classrooms.

It provoked the well-worn censorship discussion but no riots happened to support the burn-the-scripts brigade. Even in Boston they simply switched channels at 8 p.m. on Tuesday evenings to the ABC affiliate in next-door Cape Cod to watch the actors who had become the nation's favourite school kids.

John Travolta was twenty-one. He had the key to Hollywood. He had Broadway and film experience and now a weekly television series. For thousands of teenage girls, squealing, besotted and beside themselves, he was everything. He was *it* –

Hollywood's latest living-room sex symbol.

And wily Bob Le Mond kept repeating that Travolta must promote *himself* rather than Barbarino; *he* was the character not vice versa. It was another learning curve.

All the glossy women's magazines wanted this new hunk of beefcake on their covers. One quizzed him about love and sex and marriage. The best public relations reply was, 'I suppose it's all part of being on television in a good series, but it's tough talking about things I haven't even discussed with my mother.'

The confidence was there, the ambition bubbling beneath the modesty, finding the right answers. Yes, he said, he believed he was handling his success with grace: 'I suppose it's easier for me because I've had five years working up to this position.'

And he was going to continue working *up*. Zuaniuch recalled him telling her about his input into the show. 'He said: "I have the opportunity to express things in a new way every week. The cast gets together to offer ideas for the scripts. The whole concept is our own schtick."

'In one episode Vinnie comes bopping into the classroom singing with all the appropriate hand and head movements of someone very hep. Travolta explained to me, "Now that scene was initially set up very dull. But I added my own bit to the song and pulled the whole scene together. That's the kind of latitude I have.

"I love Barbarino, particularly as he's developed. I instantly knew the character in the pilot but I managed to give him more dimension as we've gone along. He used to be cool and tough but now he cries and has a lot of emotions. I find him very funny and very appealing but not very ethical and not very bright. I think it's hilarious when people call me Barbarino and react to me as if I were him. I guess it's a compliment to my acting ability. Fortunately the people in the industry know I can do something else besides Vinnie Barbarino.

"It's not as if I am unaware of what Barbarino could do for me; I knew he had the potential to be a starmaker. But acting is where my heart is. If you told me I could have millions of dollars but only if I stopped acting I wouldn't take the money. And I wouldn't have – even before *Kotter* happened for me. Acting is what I love more than anything." '

It was that way again in 1996. Memory softened his recollections of *Kotter* but he made his point about the television show: 'I had a whole career in theatre before I became famous.'

He also denied that he bought his fame portraying stereotypical New York Italians. 'Oh, my mother wouldn't allow that. The hair on her neck would stand up every time she heard that accent. It's ironic that on my first big job, *Kotter*, I played a character with an atrocious New York accent. Mom made a big point of going on the talk shows and saying that I did not speak that way in real life. I was *acting*.'

Twenty years earlier the acting – and fake Flatbushese – was paying off but fame, he said somewhat surprisingly, was beginning to bother him: 'I'd be lying if I didn't admit that I wish I could have privacy when I want it. For instance, the other night I stopped for a late supper at a restaurant. I was wearing a hat, glasses and had my collar turned up but folks at the next table recognised me and asked me for my autograph. And then once they saw somebody else do it other people started coming over. Finally, I excused myself to go to the men's room and I escaped out the back door. An actor has no privacy. That's part of the deal and there's no point in griping about it.'

Zuaniuch was surprised by this thinking. An ensemble player in what was still a fledgling, if successful, series he seemed to be swaggering before he'd even had a good walk. She was also astonished by Travolta's attitude to 'The Fonz'. The Winkler character, he told her, was 'not out of real life'. So, Vinnie Barbarino was? 'Vinnie has big plans. I think that one day he wants to be a Mafia leader. His awareness level is currently centred on sex but he's not put on. As I say Fonzie is not out of real life but Vinnie is a person. Half of him is pure innocence.'

The fan mail for Travolta/Barbarino was running at more than a thousand letters a week. He was finding the street games he used to play with Marilu Henner useful. He'd meet people 'incognito'. It was a new word for him – and a new lifestyle. He believed everyone recognized him. He got a fake stick-on beard and thick glasses from the make-up girls at ABC TV but it was hide and seek Hollywood-style. He really wanted to be found. As the fan mail increased so did his screen time and the attention. He saw himself as a Midwest version of Vinnie Barbarino – 'Vinnie has more macho but I'm brighter' – and was basking in his pedestal position as a sex symbol.

Publicly, Bob Le Mond did not exist, but he was there alright. You just had to listen closely to the sound bites. Travolta on his new status: 'That image just fell on me from nowhere. I can't imagine... girls are even fainting when I make a public appearance. It's bizarre.'

Surprise, surprise.

Chapter Eight
Bottom Line Fever

'I wouldn't know what it's like not to be an icon.' John Travolta, 1996

The months brought more fan mail and by 1977 the postbags were overflowing with up to ten thousand letters a week for John Travolta. Not Barbarino. Travolta was the blue-eyed boy in every way. He'd blink and a heart would flutter somewhere. It certainly seemed that way to the marketing 'minders', whose job was to crunch out as much mileage as they could from the new sex symbol on the network. They built the image high and grand like the skyscrapers outside their office windows. Travolta gathered more than twenty-seven million prepubescent TV followers.

In terms of media impact and Hollywood bargaining, the landmark moment that year was when he took over from 'The Fonz' as television's hottest pop icon. But even then Bob Le Mond and Lois Zetter could not realise just how deep the excitement was running for their boy.

For Travolta, teeny-bopper hearthrob, successful television 'kid', the cost of answering his fan mail – $32,500 in return postage a week – was thought excessive by ABC. He was 22 and he mused, with all the confidence of the chairman of IBM, 'I could make a million dollars this year.'

Instead, with the shrewd help of Le Mond/Zetter he did what Henry Winkler had struggled to achieve – he moved on fast from his television power base. Barbarino was power. He was 'stalked' by fans. Some in cars ran red lights, others crashed. If he was spotted on the street it was like the cartoon of the well-built blonde clicking along as the lusty driver prangs his vehicle.

Back in Englewood his parents were enjoying their son's breakthrough moments. Tuesday evenings were sacrosanct *Kotter* nights. Fans would call up Helen and Sam Travolta day and night just to say, 'We love Johnneeeeeee'.

And they did. Dwight Morrow High School, which until now had little time for the Travolta who didn't graduate, wanted to hold a John Travolta Day. He didn't think it was such a good idea. It reminded him of a very different time.

•

'When I was in Englewood I was a dumb clown not a cool clown like Barbarino. I was the sort of fool who'd do anything dumb for a laugh. Now, I'm regarded as a hero at the school. I'm trying not to let it make me crazy. Everything just eats up so much of my time. That's what my old actor friends in New York can't seem to understand. They think I don't phone or see them as often as I used to because I've "gone Hollywood" but it's just that I'm so busy. But how do you convince people you haven't "gone Hollywood"? '

With great difficulty – and little success.

The previous months had been punishing but aimed, steamrollered, at getting to this point. Bob Le Mond was learning to be a craftsman in creating a career. Lois Zetter ordered more filing cabinets and telephone lines. Travolta needed longer days. Although Le Mond-Zetter were Travolta's direct handlers they had signed him up with the William Morris Agency, the top management act with offices just a short stroll from the landmark Beverly Wilshire Hotel in Beverly Hills. The demands were constant and the fear was of stretching too thin. He wanted to be not just good but perfect at everything. Acting, dancing and singing. He'd done plenty of that in the basement, at school and on stage.

What about on record? The old RCA Records had an affiliate company, Midsong, who were keen to transfer a Top Ten TV star to the Billboard record charts. The poster image of Travolta was all tight jeans and crotch shots, the music was upbeat Doris Day, but the Travolta fans were buying. One ballad, 'Let Her In', from the predictably titled LP *John Travolta* made it to number five in the charts. Two more sickly-sweet tunes made it to the Top Forty. Somehow, Travolta found himself a Billboard hero, a true popster, and was given the music industry magazine's title of new pop male vocalist of the year.

He played down the music and said of his musical success, 'I was at about one-quarter of my ability. I said no to concerts where I could have opened for John Sebastian. So many people see you in a concert situation that you can't afford not to be great.'

His musical success – and that of John Sebastian – reflected the mid-70s culture of America. Almost all entertainment was television driven. Sebastian was a perfect example. He had left the 60s hit group the Lovin' Spoonful ('Do You Believe in Magic', 'Summer in the City') in 1968, had had a solo chart success with 'She's A Lady', and was asked to come up with a theme song for a new series called *Kotter*. Alan Sachs, the producer of *Kotter*, had mentioned to his agent Dave Bendt that he was looking for a 'Lovin' Spoonful type of song.' And, Hollywood happenstance again, Bendt also represented John Sebastian.

Sebastian recalled, 'I read a ten-page synopsis of the storyline and later a first draft of the first episode. It seemed to me the relationship the teacher had with his students was not unlike the relationship I had with this producer – antagonistic friendship. I wrote a song one afternoon that was ghastly and threw it away. I wrote another song that was *Welcome Back.* '

Alan Sachs and everyone else involved in the project loved the song enough to change the title of the television series to *Welcome Back, Kotter.* It was lucky. The only word Sebastian could find to rhyme with Kotter was otter. He'd gnawed at that long enough before producing the song that became a number one hit in America on 8 May 1976. That was exactly ten weeks after Rhythm Heritage's 'The Theme from S.W.A.T.' had become the first television theme song to get to number one in the American charts.

Twenty years later Travolta experienced a musical deja vu. He had followed up his first album with *Can't Let You Go* (from which his 'Slow Dancing' track made the music charts) but, of course, it had nothing of the later impact of the records from *Saturday Night Fever* and *Grease.* In 1996 'Greased Lightnin'' was among the most requested songs at American weddings. And selling well on the back of the Travolta movie resurrection was the album *John Travolta: Greased Lightnin'* brought out by Charly Records at a knockdown price. The fact-tinted liner notes told us, 'Travolta was a star on record before Hollywood beckoned.'

In January 1996, Travolta found himself on VH1 television, a goofy 70s Travolta appearing in re-runs of his two Dick Clark *American Bandstand* performances. The company's vice president of music programming, Lee Chesnut, said: 'We'd love a new video of Travolta. It wouldn't matter if the video or song were good or bad. We'd play the hell out of it. With movies like *Get Shorty, Broken Arrow* and *Phenomenon* he's hot and that's what brings in the people, which is what everybody wants.'

Travolta's career soared on the first wave of music-industry hype. He got the Tom Jones treatment, the knickers and bras thrown during personal appearance crushes and local policemen made extra money moonlighting as 'Travolta Security'. It was not so much the records that drove the anxious, curious fans to his public appearances: they wanted an up close look at the pin-up who was beamed into their homes every week on TV.

But it was not enough for Travolta. At the time much was made of him turning his back on the music business, personal appearances and lucrative television offers which he could have accepted during the hiatus from *Welcome Back, Kotter.* He even rejected Carly Simon, (with whom he would be romantically linked following her break-up with James Taylor) who offered him a song and to help produce his third album. He dismissed it, apparently disdainfully at the time with, 'I have a good voice and want it to be a class act.'

Travolta seemed to want to get back to his roots on the stage, which was what Harold Kennedy thought when he hired Travolta and his sisters Ellen, then 37, and Annie, then 25, in a Travolta family package deal. But for Kennedy at least, Travolta's failure to get time off from *Kotter* to make *Days of Heaven* for Terence Malick turned out to be a blessing.

Kennedy and his production partner, Skipp Lynch, were planning a summer stock run of *Bus Stop* – the 1956 movie version of William Inge's play about the showgirl and coy cowboy had starred Marilyn Monroe and Don Murray – but, only weeks away from rehearsals, still needed a leading man.

' "You must get hold of John Travolta," ' Kennedy recalled Lynch telling him.

"John who?", I asked.

' "John Travolta, he's Barbarino."

' "Who the hell is Barbarino?"

' "He's on a very successful television show."

' "Is he hot? "

' "Very". '

Kennedy went on, 'I had never heard of him but I decided to write the name down and ask a few people. Nobody I asked had ever heard of John Travolta either…Skipp doesn't give up easily. He called back a few days later. "What have you done about John Travolta?" he asked.

"Oh," I said, stalling, "he's the one that plays Valentino"

"Not Valentino," said Skipp patiently, "Barbarino. I've got his agent's number," said Skipp. "Call them right away." And he gave me the number of the William Morris office.

"Who do I talk to about John Travolta?" I asked.

"John who?" they said

'We finally got that all straight and they put me in touch with my old friend Ed Robbins, who was the first person I had contacted who knew who John Travolta was. I asked him if John might be interested in doing some summer stock.'

The response came back very rapidly. Yes, John Travolta would like to play in William Inge's *Bus Stop* and he wanted his two sisters to play two of the leading female parts.

'That really chilled my blood. I didn't know whether he could act, let alone his two sisters. I saw them in the beginning sort of as twin albatrosses around my neck. Turned out, happily, that I was wrong.

'But I did think *Bus Stop* was a good idea. By then I had seen John on a segment of *Welcome Back, Kotter* and he was perfect casting for Bo.

'The first offer we made of John Travolta to all of the summer managers was a unanimous turndown. "John who?" was a gentle reaction. In some quarters it was even suggested that I had made up the name. But by now I knew a lot more about John Travolta myself and I was convinced that we had a potential blockbuster.

Then when the first day of rehearsal on *Bus Stop* was less than ten days away I received a call early one morning from Lois Zetter saying that John would not be able to do *Bus Stop*. He had already signed his contracts but that didn't seem to matter.

'He had been offered a picture which it was literally impossible for him to turn down. It was a glorious script and was sure to make him a major film star. The director wanted him and John to do it more than he ever had anything else in his life. So it was going to have to be worked out, no matter however.

'I hung up in a state of shock.

'There is an Equity rule, or at least there was at that time, whereby a star can buy out of a contract three weeks prior to the first rehearsal by paying the management the exact amount of his contractual salary. This has been much complained about by the managers, and it may have been rectified by now.

'When I hung up from Lois Zetter I felt that she had represented John fairly and strongly, but I also sensed that she herself was genuinely disturbed over the situation.

'I called her back and said, "we have no time for screaming or shrieking or threatening or wailing. What can we do to salvage at least part of this situation?"

' "What do you want me to do?" Lois asked.

' "I want you to call this boy right away," I said. "Tell him I don't want him to lose the picture, but I want him to stay with the play as long as he can before the picture starts. That would obviously include the first two weeks. And every single day longer that he can stay, even if it is only for a partial week."

'She called me back in half an hour.

' "John says he's terribly sorry for all the trouble he has caused. And he will stay with the play as long as he can. He will not go back to California until the night before shooting starts."

'On opening night it was apparent that we had a bonanza. Families came with their teenage children from distances of 200 miles. When John strode onto the stage halfway through the first act the theatre came apart.

'Now, what about that picture John was supposed to do? He never did it. It haunted us all summer long. It was on again, off again every other day.

It was obvious to me very soon that the *Welcome Back, Kotter* people were never going to give John the releases he would have needed to do the film.

'He offered them literally a fortune for his release. He would have been in hock for the next couple of years.

'But the *Kotter* people said no. John cried on the phone. And the director cried on the phone.

'John didn't find out definitely until the day before the opening in Falmouth when he had flown back to California that he could not do the picture.

'John was philosophical about the loss. For about a week he was very quiet about it and obviously keenly disappointed. Then one day he said to me:

"Harold, you know why I didn't get the picture? Because it was wrong. I was wrong to try and get it. I was being unfair to you. And to *Bus Stop*. And to *Kotter*. And when things are wrong they don't work out. And they shouldn't."

'Whatever disappointment he felt must have been quickly appeased when he got back to California. He was immediately signed by Robert Stigwood Organisation to a three-picture $1 million contract.

'The first film was *Saturday Night Fever* which won Travolta an award from the National Board of review as "best actor of the year" and an Academy Award nomination.

'The difference in John between the time he left me after *Bus Stop* and the time I met him after the completion of *Saturday Night Fever* is enormous. It is perhaps best illustrated by the difference in his behind.

'I had first become aware of John's behind in clippings from *Midwest* describing his personal appearances before thousands of fans in auditoriums, shopping centres, supermarkets, and so on. Invariable mention was made of the fact that the young lady fans would ask John to turn around so they could look at his behind. This fascinated me and seemed something quite new in the annals of idolatry.

' "John," I said to him one day after we had gotten to know each other, "I don't understand the mystique of your behind. I don't mean to be rude, but you have what I would describe as a totally utilitarian behind. It looks very comfortable to sit on. But decorative it definitely is not."

' "It is kind of chunky," he said. "And you're right. But as George Bernard Shaw once said to someone who booed one of his plays, 'I agree with you, my friend, but who are you and I against so many?' "

'But nonetheless when I met John a year later, the behind, like everything else, had been trimmed down to superstar status.

'Chunkiness is not for John – in his body, his performances, or his life. Everything is streamlined to perfection. That's why he's on his way to being a superstar if he isn't one already. And a richly deserving one...'

Chapter Nine
Carrie Forward

'It was an easy reality.'

John Travolta in 1977, on his oral sex scene in *Carrie*

T ravolta was a fledgling television star, Nancy Allen was a graduate of Cool Whip Toppings commercials and Brian De Palma had directed a string of shock-horror films when fate put them together in a movie that would change all their lives, as well as that of the freckled, snub-nosed actress Sissy Spacek who had the title role of 'Carrie'.

De Palma went on to make landmark films like *Dressed to Kill* with Michael Caine and Angie Dickinson, *Blow Out* working again with Travolta, *Scarface* with Al Pacino and Michelle Pfeiffer, *Body Double* with Melanie Griffith, *Casualties of War* with Sean Penn, *The Bonfire of the Vanities* with Tom Hanks, Bruce Willis and Melanie Griffith and *The Untouchables* with Robert De Niro, Sean Connery and Kevin Costner, but in 1976 he was desperate.

'All my best friends in the business – Marty Scorsese, George Lucas, Steven Spielberg – had already made it in a huge way and there was I after eight or nine pictures still struggling. When *Carrie* came along I pleaded to be allowed to direct it.'

The first of Stephen King's eerie, page-turning blockbusters to be adapted by Hollywood, tells of the teenage school outcast whose classmates elect her Prom Queen so they can mock and humiliate her even more. In an opening shower scene, she is ridiculed for her fear of menstruation and things get even bloodier when *Carrie* unleashes her telekinetic powers. Her scary skills would bulge a library of 'X-files'.

Spacek had made her cinema impact in 1972 in *Badlands* as a 15-year-old infatuated with Martin Sheen's on-the-run psychotic young killer. For *Carrie* she won her first Oscar nomination and was named Best Actress by America's National Society of Film Critics. However, she had not been De Palma's first choice for the role. He was ambivalent about her until she 'absolutely floored me' with her screen test. After that he said he had no hesitation.

He also took instantly to two young players who were to be Carrie's classmates: Travolta and Nancy Allen.

'I think Brian liked us best,' said Travolta adding, 'We would go out of our way to entertain him.'

Travolta's role was as a nasty piece of work called Billy Nolan, who is engineered to take Carrie to the prom. He just happens to be waylaid, so to speak, by Nancy Allen, as a playground bitch and Carrie's prime tormentor. She engages in enthusiastic oral sex with Travolta in the front of a car. Travolta was later asked about the raunchy sex scene and – without intended puns – replied, 'It was something that had happened to me in real life. It wasn't hard for me because it was an easy reality.'

There were more intimidating scenes and he was still in an oral mind frame when he talked about one. 'I had to simulate the bludgeoning of a pig and those things don't mind taking a bite out of you.'

He survived. He and Nancy Allen lived close to each other off Sunset Boulevard and often turned up for work together. Instantly, they were labelled a couple and it was presumed that their movie sex scenes had gone on after filming stopped. No, they said, they were simply a carpool. Indeed, they said, Travolta had played Cupid to Allen and De Palma.

De Palma took his young actors out to dinner. He recalled telling them of the cruel cinema world: 'The lesson to learn is that as successful and powerful as you can become you can still be out-manoeuvred. In an industry filled with half-truths and inflated praise and all kinds of false signals you have to have a very clear idea of how you are actually regarded.

'If you get sucked in you can get wiped out. I've seen a lot of people levelled because they misread signals: they thought they were being offered a three-picture deal when they were actually being put out to pasture.

'I didn't say this with any bitterness. It's simply the business. Don't expect good faith. There's no such thing.'

How much of this penetrated Travolta is too long ago for him to know. But he was, as ever, observing his companions personalities and gestures. Travolta the human sponge soaking up everything with the pasta. He certainly caught De Palma's feelings and remembered, 'I told Nancy, "He really likes you." '

Three months after *Carrie* was completed De Palma and Allen began dating and after a long bi-coastal romance they married in 1979.

Back at *Kotter* things were not so friendly.

Travolta had called Gabe Kaplan 'a sweet, sensitive man' but as *Kotter* ran successfully into its second year it was clear that the kids were getting more rewards than the teacher. Visitors to the set in North Hollywood, which with its high fencing felt like a compound, reported it as a 'cold war' zone. Robert Hegyes wanted out of his contract. Ron Palillo and Gabe Kaplan were not talking.

'Kaplan didn't seem to get along with Travolta either. He was sort of sneering at Travolta. He was sneering at everyone,' said an ABC producer who worked on the series. 'Kaplan was very isolated from the rest of the class. In fact, he went off by himself the minute the breaks came. The rest of the cast sat in a group but the only time he talked to them was when they were rehearsing their lines.

Actress Marcia Strassman (with whose sister julie Travolta had a fluttering romance) played Kaplan's wife in the series and recalled the atmosphere. 'It got so strained I didn't speak to Gabe off camera. It was "hello" and that was it. It was tough on everyone.'

But as well as the glory and the regular pay cheques they all had contracts. Michael Eisner was then an ABC TV programming executive. He recalled the determination with which Travolta tried to free himself to do *Days of Heaven*. ABC adamantly wanted him to do the more prosaic *The Boy in the Plastic Bubble*. That, to a disdainful Travolta, was a TV movie-of-the-week.

It was getting tough everywhere.

'*Days of Heaven* was a kind of supersubjective *Easy Rider* and the part was very theatrical and very deep, all about the Search for Self, so naturally Travolta was determined to play it,' said Eisner. He said the incident was at that point 'the biggest battle of my career'. He went on:

'He wanted to do the film and that was that. The battle nearly blew him out of the water but in the end the network got its way.'

Travolta was petulant. 'As a kid I was a seductive brat. I loved affection, loved to be held, hugged and kissed.' But ABC TV weren't doing any kissing or hugging. He couldn't understand. He wasn't getting what he wanted. When his father built planes for him in the backyard, he asked for them to fly. His father made them. What was wrong with Eisner? James Komak?

Randal Kleiser began his distinguished career as a director in television and was drawn to 'social' stories. He followed 1975 *Dawn: Portrait of a Teenaged Runaway* with *The Boy in the Plastic Bubble*. It could have simply been a forerunner of all the disease-of-the-week movies which were to cover the airwaves like a nasty virus for the next couple of decades.

Instead, it was a moving tale of a boy born without natural immunities. He's allergic to *everything*. He is forced to live in a germ-free artificial environment, sealed in a bubble. He watches normal life literally pass him by.

ABC regarded the TV movie as a strong vehicle for Travolta and he was paid nearly $750,000, in a breathlessly reported deal.

For actress Diana Hyland it was just another TV movie. Been there, done that, could have been her attitude. It wasn't. She was a highly-regarded professional, a veteran of the stage and movies; she'd co-starred with Paul Newman in Broadway's *Sweet Bird of Youth* and in *The Chase* in 1966, which had a stellar cast including Marlon Brando, Janice Rule, Robert Redford and Jane Fonda. It was Redford's breakthrough movie and one that would become a cult.

She was also familiar from the daytime soap *Young Dr Malone* and *Peyton Place* (1964–1968), the mother of all television soap operas, where she worked with Mia Farrow, Ryan O'Neal and Barbara Parkin. She was Mr Winter the minister's wife who had a penchant for drinks stiffer than sherry and a nymphomaniac's taste for similar men. This was an actress who had worked with and knew the big stars. She was not easily intimidated by other people's fame.

Born Diana Genter in January 1936 she was a Midwest girl from the outskirts of Cleveland, Ohio. She got the acting bug early and her clean-cut, blonde good looks got her stage work in New York in her late teens. The big breakthrough role never came but she worked consistently in good and small, big and bad parts and all stages in between. She had been married and divorced from actor Joe Goodson when she went to work on *The Boy in the Plastic Bubble*. She had her own son – three-year-old curly-haired Zachary at home with an adoring housekeeper from Salvador.

Hyland had that agelessness that happens on camera. The lighting helps but her bone structure did more. While she was filming *Boy in the Plastic Bubble* her agent signed her on for an episode of *Happy Days*. She was to play a character half her age – a girlfriend of, ironically, The Fonz. And here she was working with the opposition. Hold that: falling in love with the opposition.

Travolta was the young and good-looking star of this particular project. He was also nice. The perpetual charm kicked in from day one.

But Travolta found something else happening to him. His attitude to women until then had been to be kind, cavalier. Although he would deny it, 'There was a minimum of heartbreaking I could do because from the start I'd say: "Hey, this is the situation."

'I am always more open, loving, complimentary and adoring to the person who comes with built-in barriers – someone I know there's no future with. When I know there's an absolute future I get more restrictive. I don't let that person know how much I care because it could develop into something more serious and permanent. I was always scared of that.'

He soon discovered that Diana Hyland was easy to like. She had 'baggage': a three-year-old son. And she was older, 40 to his 22.

She was playing his mother in the television movie, but it didn't make any difference.

'On the first meeting I was just incredibly attracted to this woman. I saw the whole picture in the first ten words – depth, intelligence, beauty, perceptiveness. She'd gone through a rough marriage, a lot of career ups and downs and had come out at peace with herself. It was very sexy. The most important things in her life were the relationships.

'She really savoured the people around her. At the time I was open, just fooling around with a couple of little affairs. I had almost decided to quit looking for someone special and then she came along and was so dynamic I knew I had to spend time with her.

'She broke my heart from the start but it took a month before I decided to be with her. We were like two maniacs talking all the time on the set of *Bubble* but it took a month to become romantic.

'When she said it didn't matter whether or not we were together romantically – that she could have me either way, sexually or just as a friend – that was the deciding moment. That was when I realized she appreciated me as a person rather than just as a young stud.

'Then I said, "Alright, I can do this." At that time in my life I was in the middle of complete hysteria and she was quite an influence. The relationship gave me a calming quality.'

Naturally, Randal Kleiser, their director, spotted the relationship first. He saw it on close-focus camera and off-screen. 'It was clear they wanted each other. I don't think any sort of barriers would have stopped them.'

Kleiser encountered an absurdly happy Travolta, but also a perfectionist. 'John's dedicated, but when he gets to know you he can be a lot of fun. On *Bubble* I'll always remember what he improvised when this boy born without immunities, sealed up until the age of eighteen, is finally released into the world. In that scene John ran outdoors, picked up handfuls of earth and, in the ecstasy of his first freedom, rubbed himself with it – a really great touch and very physical.

'When he works John broods endlessly about whether he's good. He'd call me late at night to ask what went well that day. At the same time he'd keep the atmosphere on the set very light if he thought others needed that – he felt it was his duty. He can be a comedian at these times…'

But Hollywood – in the sense of Travolta's camp – didn't see the joke. Indeed, they saw a problem with what was making Travolta so happy. Here was a pre-teen and teeny-bopper sex god romancing a woman who, in their terms, was 'some old lady.' And this was no sneak romance, this was capital letter LOVE.

The media focus on Travolta/Barbarino was so strong that the relationship would have been revealed even if he and Diana had tried to disguise it. In fact a gossip column was going to print a story about them which provoked them to co-operate with a journalist on a celebrity magazine article.

It was not heart-revealing material. Travolta said, 'I've had different girlfriends but always on a casual level. That's unsettling. I know now what I want and need.'

Diana Hyland said, 'John's not like many people I've ever met. He's mature, sensitive and giving, very easy to be with. My son Zachary loves Johnny and Johnny loves him.' And – the *Kotter* hysteria of the day must be understood – she made a point of adding, 'John's the antithesis of Barbarino.'

That in turn provoked Travolta to declare, 'I'm not a playboy, slick with the women, putting them in their place – all that number.'

It was only later in their tragically short relationship that they opened up more but that was usually at dinner with friends and family, especially Travolta's sister Ellen who was similar in age to Diana, had pounded the audition beat with her and who handled the family public relations for her younger brother's love affair.

Diana looked jounger than she was, with her wide, bright smile and shoulder-length cascade of curls. When they went out publicly she would link her arms around Travolta's right arm and her eyes were always protectively on him. They spent almost all their time together, Travolta playing father to Zachary and 'house' at his high-rise apartment in West Hollywood, where a percentage of the $450 monthly rent went on a security guard and electronic garage gates. He had a yellow Mercedes 450SL, a classic 1955 Thunderbird and a Honda 350 motorbike tucked in corner parking spots as far away from other drivers' scratching doors as possible.

He liked his new role as man-of-the-house. He told everybody, 'This is the first time I've ever been in love. All my love affairs with young girls – I've had four or five going at the same time – were nothing more than affairs. With Diana I'm settled.'

Diana Hyland tried to stay in the shadows, believing that was best for his career. In one comment she said, 'We have a lovely relationship, really lovely. John is very much older than he appears but, anyway, age makes no difference to us. I don't think that in today's world anyone considers it unusual for people of different age groups to have a relationship. It happens all the time.'

Travolta's career was continuing to flourish. *Bubble* had been a ratings success and he had received impressive reviews. Boosted by his popularity from *Kotter* and the music charts his name was billed directly after Sissy Spacek's on *Carrie*. The movie was a runaway success – he and Diana attended the Hollywood première together. He felt 'a lot' of that success was due to him and said so often and publicly. De Palma and the rest of those involved let him have his day although Piper Laurie (Carrie's mother in the movie) mumbled dissent.

A year before she was cast in *The Boy in the Plastic Bubble* Diana Hyland had undergone a mastectomy. She had the routine five-year wait for a cancer all-clear but had been told that that would be a formality: the surgery to remove her left breast had removed all the malignant cells. She had cosmetic surgery to make her figure camera friendly.

Travolta knew all about the cancer. He wasn't frightened by it. When he was seventeen his mother had had surgery and he had insisted on changing her bandages and applying salve to her open wound. He did it without embarrassment. And his mother had got well. He was confident that his lover had beaten cancer.

Diana Hyland was cast opposite Dick Van Patten, the cheery, chubby film and television veteran and real-life family patriarch, as the parents of the big brood in *Eight Is Enough* which ran on ABC TV for six years from 1977. It brought her sacks of fan mail.

Travolta was at the centre of a colourful world, one surrounded by rainbows, driven by ambition and avarice, and splendid showmanship.

Glamour is never more than a handshake away from Allan Carr. He was caviar and champagne to Bob Le Mond's meat and potatoes. Travolta was on both their menus. Carr, a furniture dealer's son born in Chicago in 1941, had arrived in Hollywood a quarter of a century later intent on capturing the town.

Big and round apart from intermittent dieting (one of the few people who could ever go on a diet 'spree') he had been involved with Australian entrepreneur Robert Stigwood in adapting the stage musical *Grease* for the movies. A personal manager (clients included Ann-Margret and Marisa Berenson who would later 'date' Travolta) he was a master of the grand gesture. For years Carr would conclude any sentence involving Travolta and *Grease* with 'I was the one who said, "Put him in the movie". '

The real story was that he and Stigwood wanted Henry Winkler as the leading man in the *Grease* film but Winkler didn't want the job. 'He said the part was too much like Fonzie,' said Carr. 'It was about that time that Travolta showed up in *Kotter*. I thought he was terrific.'

So did Stigwood. The Robert Stigwood Organisation (RSO was the record label) had entertainment involvement worldwide. Stigwood had signed the Bee Gees to a lucrative contract in 1971. He had also launched the careers of Cream (with Eric Clapton) and Blind Faith. He had gusted into the London theatre scene in 1968 presenting a kid called Andrew Lloyd-Webber and his partner Tim Rice's *Jesus Christ Superstar*. He had also produced, with the help of Kenneth Tynan, the naughty *Oh, Calcutta*.

He has also been responsible for the landmark television series *Till Death Us Do*

Part and *Steptoe and Son* and had also licensed their American counterparts.

Stigwood was always impatient to get on, to move on from recording and establish himself in movies. But there was a timing problem with the movie *Grease* in the competition that existed between stage and screen versions. A couple of decades later a movie of Andrew Lloyd-Webber's *Phantom of the Opera* was still waiting to be made because of threats to the 'house' of franchised touring companies around the world. So it was with *Grease*. No movie, said the contracts, until the spring of 1978.

Eventually, the Stigwood Organisation and Travolta's team settled on a $1 million fee for Travolta to make a trio of movies: *Saturday Night Fever, Grease* and the 'adult' film *Moment by Moment.* He would also receive a heavy profit share of all earnings and merchandising including recordings. The deal cemented Travolta's financial future, but all the parties involved took a gamble that the movies would hit big, for the upfront fees wouldn't cover Travolta's television-movie earning power, as proved by *The Boy in the Plastic Bubble.* But Le Mond was always thinking ahead, moving his protege on and up. Career, career, career was his mantra.

But Travolta's mainspring was Diana, and it was she on whom he relied for advice on his next step.

'She gave me the confidence. She was the one who persuaded me to play Tony Manero in *Fever*,' said Travolta when later he talked movingly of his lost love.

' " Do it!," she told me. "It will be the making of you. It's got all the colours..." '

It might have been the end of their rainbow, but it was the beginning of his as a superstar.

Chapter Ten
Dirty Pool

'You're going to act like
nobody else of your generation.'

Diana Hyland to John Travolta, March 1977

We will never know who was the ultimate puppet master or mistress on the embryo *Saturday Night Fever*. However, its genesis lay in writer Nik Cohn's long feature article in the glossy and 1970s ground-breaking *New York* magazine, which specialised in in-depth investigations and fine writing about social and cultural issues. But 'culture' did not, according to editor Clay Feldman, necessarily have to follow the high arts.

London-born Cohn's piece was headlined 'Tribal Rites of the New Saturday Night' and was published in June 1976. It focused on the lives beneath the glamorous veneer of the disco clubs of Brooklyn. These were blue collar hang-outs at weekends, places where the workers could discard their overalls for the glitter and glam of disco. It was a world in which you strutted your stuff, sweating for dance-floor fame and oh-so-casual sex. The only Madonna around was in chapel not the pop charts. Girls were boy-toys.

Cohn's central character, 'Vincent', came alive once a week, on Saturday nights. The movie's Tony Manero was a hybrid of Vincent and the moviemaking art. He was the master of the dance floor, the disco dervish of the flashing lights, the 19-year-old with all his hopes and ambitions in his toes. He believed they could march him into a future.

Stigwood said he sensed the movie immediately: music, youth and sex. Lois Zetter says Bob Le Mond read the piece and thought it could be turned into a perfect vehicle for Travolta. But on Allan Carr's insistence that it had been his influence that secured the part for Travolta, she demurred:

'That's what *he* says. But John was obviously ready. And it would be silly to think that Allan was the only one to recognise it. John was ready. He was probably the only one not to fully know that.'

Travolta had signed the *Fever* contracts on the strength of Cohn's article, Stigwood's spiel and, of course, Diana's advice.

Travolta and Diana Hyland talked for hours about his career. She could always fall back on experience, on the parts she'd rejected and the ones she'd taken under sufferance and resented; also she had accepted roles simply to pay the rent. Earlier Travolta had vowed never to do that. But it was a teenage thing, pride. He was now thinking as a family man.

As he read the script Travolta was hesitant about *Fever*. He was shy of anything that he did not think he could deliver perfectly. And to him Tony Manero felt like an older, unpleasant Vinnie Barbarino. 'All I could see in him was the tough hostility. It was Diana who turned my head around.

'I was reading the script. It was late. I kept frowning as I read. Diana had this way of studying me, smiling, very sharp, funny but very compassionate. When I finished she took the script into another room. An hour later she ran back. "Baby", she shouted, "you're going to be great in this!" I dumbly asked why. She was striding around the room very excited. "Baby, he's got all the colours, he's miles from what you've played."

' "He's furious because he feels the excitement of the whole world when he dances. Staying in Brooklyn is torture for him. Baby, he cares. Catholicism has mixed this boy up; he tries on his brother's priest collar in front of the mirror – what a moment for an actor!

' "And he grows up, he gets out of Brooklyn. Okay, maybe all that isn't in the script but you'll know how to put it there." '

A less excited Travolta rebutted, 'I told her, "Diana, he's also king of the disco. I'm not that good a dancer." She said, "Baby, you'll learn."

'It was like an order. The next day I began three months of intensive disco-dancing training.'

He spent three hours a day on his dancing. Then he had to get 'inside' the New York singles scene, the world of Tony Manero and his glitter wardrobe. It meant commuting between Los Angeles and New York, between Diana Hyland and Tony Manero.

Travolta was a regular on the American Airlines 'red-eye'. Never one to lose himself in novels he would flip through the celebrity magazines like *People*, and doze on the flights. He liked the big submarine-type sandwiches they served instead of hot meals.

The two lovers had spent weekends away in the California desert resort of Palm Springs and up in the mountains of Big Bear where you can sunbathe by the swimming pool and ski in the same afternoon. Often Zachary was with them. There were also visits to New York and Englewood. Travolta's parents would fly out to see them and the whole family would stay at Ellen Travolta's 'New Jersey annex' near Palm Springs.

'I had more fun with Diana than I ever had in my life and the odd thing is, just before we met I thought I would never have a successful relationship. She told me that she too had thought the same thing. Then, bam!'

The next *bam* was brutal. Diana thought she had caught flu. A bad attack. She was also brought down by constant back trouble, aches and pains throughout Christmas of 1976. In the New Year she received her death sentence: cancer had spread throughout her body. Tumours were riding down her spine. It was hard to believe. To begin with she looked fine, but her body swiftly collapsed. Radiotherapy became too hard for her to bear and recover from. She was only marking time in hospital. Travolta was in New York, filming and they talked on the phone but she had to gather what remained of her strength for the calls.

When Edward and Mary Genter flew out from Ohio, they were shocked by her appearance and couldn't hide it. Their daughter was wasting away. 'She was sick but she really didn't want to burden the people she loved,' said her mother. 'She was still worried about others, about Zachary and John. She was very brave.'

She wanted to die in her own bed and Travolta and her parents eventually took her home. She told people around her not to fuss but, although she was so weak, she never stopped caring about her appearance – she wore her favourite pink nightgown and had her hair washed and curled. By then she was only sipping distilled water and taking morphine for the pain. She slipped in and out of consciousness, but when she was awake she was remarkably lucid.

Travolta flew out West on 26 March 1977, and within twenty-four hours she was dead in his arms.

'She was very unhappy in hospital and we took her to her little Spanish adobe home. To be honest, our last conversation was about what we were going to have for dinner. I went out and got Japanese food or something and when I brought it back she'd already gone into the unconscious stage.

'Her cancer had been in remission. There had been hope. Today she would have been OK. The 70s were rough on women with that particular problem.'

It was only weeks since they had been house-hunting, planning a home for themselves and Zachary and celebrating their planned engagement with a pre-honeymoon trip to Rio de Janeiro. Now, Brazil seemed on another planet. All he had left of that dream was the white linen suit they had chosen together for him to wear on the holiday. He had been with Diana Hyland for just seven months. It seemed like a lifetime.

The day before she died she had told him, 'I am going now but you are going to have this work.'

On that grey, overcast Sunday evening in March with the blanket of cloud from the Pacific blowing in over Westwood, he says he felt 'the breath go out of her'. She was 41. He was a very grown-up 23: I was with her all through the night before she died. I held her, touched her, all through those hours.'

'The speed of it all was a shock for him,' says Ellen Travolta. 'He was devastated not only by the loss but because there was nothing he could do. Until Diana's death John felt in control of his own fate and had never experienced anything tragic.

'He suddenly felt helpless, aware of his own mortality. Later he confided to me, "If Diana can do it, so can I." It made him lose his fear of death. He was never the same. Something like that changes you forever.'

His mother said, 'He didn't know Diana was sick when he fell in love but he stuck with her when he did know.

'He managed to convince his associates that her frequent visits to the hospital were because of "back trouble".

'Sometimes he even managed to convince himself that they were.'

Almost two decades on, in some sense Diana Hyland is still with him. 'The qualities that drew me to her? Put aside her being talented and sexy and one of the most beautiful people I'd ever seen, she had a depth to her, a generosity of spirit that was extraordinary.

'I gave her great joy in the last months of her life. I always feel she is with me – I mean her intentions are. Diana always wanted the world for me in every possible way.'

Her death, and what Ellen Travolta calls a 'bittersweet time' for him found him more and more drawn to Scientology. He attended self-help seminars almost daily. 'The family respects his practice of Scientology,' said Ellen. 'None of us do it though I and a few others took courses which lasted about twelve hours in 1994. Basically it took things that were on your mind and helped put them in order. I really enjoyed it.'

Her brother is glad of the family support and understanding. 'Scientology helped me so much back then. I don't know why people are afraid of it. It's given me a better quality of life and a hope for mankind. And a better sense of survival.'

He needed to hold on then during what he would later call 'the hardest ten weeks of my life.'

He had Diana and Zachary to think about and *Saturday Night Fever*. 'I would have married Diana. I would have been over the moon if we had had a baby. I would have done anything in this world for that not to have happened. It was a disaster and it will always be a disaster. If I had not had the work I might have gone crazy.'

Diana and he had made plans for Travolta to adopt Zachary but the little boy went to his father and in 1996 was living in a quiet suburb of Los Angeles asking for privacy. The past was past.

Diana Hyland was cremated with tears but no fuss. Later, at a memorial gathering at her home, Travolta wore the white suit planned for Rio. He never wore it again. Like a bridal gown it was wrapped and boxed and sent to Englewood. He went East too and back to work.

On the set of *Saturday Night Fever* the cast and crew didn't know what to say. Director John Badham, who had taken over from original director John *Rocky* Avilsden, said: 'John didn't want people to feel sorry for him. After the funeral he had the hardest scenes to do, the scenes with the family. But he was very professional and plunged in. The entire cast and crew felt terrible. They gave a large donation to the Damon Runyon Cancer Fund which deeply touched John.'

Travolta had leased an apartment in Manhattan below Carly Simon and James Taylor. It was on plush Central Park West – not bad for a New Jersey boy – and neighbours also included Mia Farrow, Liv Ullman and British movie director John Schlesinger. He had lost interest in socialising but one evening he needed company.

He left his apartment and knocked on the Simon/Taylor door. He found Taylor strumming his guitar and happy over the birth of his son Ben. Nevertheless, the couple were having difficult personal times. They and Travolta talked, shared their problems and became good friends. Taylor was a *Kotter* fan – he even knew some Barbarino rap – and both he and his wife also understood the pressures of stardom. It was, however, to work that Travolta turned to fill the terrible gap.

He rode out to Brooklyn for location work in some of the tough areas where 'dirty pool' meant life stealing from you what you wanted most. For the Tony Maneros it was just getting out of Brooklyn. For Travolta, it was getting the pain out of his head. 'By choice I didn't have a day off. I rehearsed the dance numbers on weekends. For twelve weeks I was up at five every morning and didn't get home until ten at night.'

He also worked with a Scientology 'auditor' on helping himself through the stress, and he hired Jimmy Gambina, a former boxer who had prepared Sylvester Stallone for *Rocky* as his trainer. He laughed. 'Used Sly's trainer. Had to lose 20lbs. Lost 22. Got a whole new body out of it.'

And a haircut. And an 18-hour-day attitude. John Badham says he had never 'really watched' Travolta on television. His star's potential was unknown to him. He realised as soon as filming began:

'I'd never seen anyone so dedicated. It was very exciting to watch the dailies and realise that we had a huge new star on our hands. His magnetism amazed me. So did the fact that any actor could be so driven.

'In Brooklyn we had real trouble shooting the movie because the crowds John drew were huge but he couldn't have been less on a "star" trip. Getting the movie right obsessed him. His head was always buried in the script and he came to every one of the dailies – some stars don't bother. In rehearsal he'd constantly improvise trying new pieces of business, stretching himself.

'Remember in the picture when his dancing partner asks if he'd invented a particular step himself and he answers, "Yeah, I saw it on TV and *then* I made it up" That was John's own invention and a great touch.

'Of course, he did *know* that the movie could be his biggest shot.'

So far that had involved Vinnie Barbarino. *Kotter* was also still on the Travolta agenda. The contract said so and Travolta put on a brave face, although he had lost all interest in the TV spin-off *Vinnie*. That was then. *Fever* was now.

'I love slipping into the role of Barbarino. It's just that I have to do it so often. I can deal with it as long as I have the freedom to do movies,' he said diplomatically at the time.

His 'team', particularly lawyer Frederick Gaines, were the ones dealing with it. He concentrated on Tony Manero. 'I had to work at him. Take Barbarino. On paper Vinnie read real dumb. He could have been played as just a farcical jerk but I went to school with guys like him and I've always been an observer of human behaviour.

'I remember a guy who was just like Vinnie, all macho bravado on the outside but secretly very innocent, naive. I worked on every *Kotter* script with that character in mind, let these subtler colours come through. It took me a while. I'm not easy to please when it comes to my work. I'm very hard on myself. I worked on Tony in *Fever* the same way.'

He worked very hard for he had an important legacy to fulfil. Diana Hyland was with him. 'To say there was no woman like Diana – that's cliché but so what? There *wasn't* anyone like her. She was a real woman. Her femininity knocked me out yes she was so bright…ironic! She could be a tease. Her humour was both funky and very elegant and it was always there.

'And she was on Broadway and so on a long time, and what really made her thrilled and me too was that later in her career she found a whole new audience in television. The humour of hers finally came into everybody's living room. The mail she got – she was loved. I guess that's also a cliché.

'When Diana was dying she smiled and said, "You're going to carry on what I can't, baby. You're going to act like nobody else of your generation! Now remember that, baby, remember it."

'But it's the way she said "baby" I always remember first.'

Chapter Eleven
What Did You Say Your Name Was?

'Here's a rule that Hollywood lives by: There's no need to be nice to anybody on spec.' Hollywood writer Rafael Taglesias, 1996

The story that became the film *Saturday Night Fever* involved Nik Cohn in months of research around the disco clubs. It was a different world with its own codes and dress. Cohn wrote, 'The new generation takes few risks: it graduates, looks for a job, endures. And once a week on Saturday night it explodes.'

The moviemakers also did their research. Location manager Lloyd Kaufman worked for weeks in pre-production looking for a club to film the dance sequences. Cohn had focused his story on the 2001 Odyssey Club in Bay Ridge. So did the film. 'We looked at every disco in Manhattan, Brooklyn and Queens and even considered converting a loft to our own specifications before deciding on 2001,' said Kaufman adding, 'That was really always our first choice but we wanted to consider all the possibilities to make sure we were right.'

The story was of the kids of that moment, that generation. There was a 50s jukebox feel, a world where aspirations were anchored in television. Travolta fan Pauline Kael described them as 'part of the post-Watergate working-class generation with no heroes except in TV-showbiz-lands; they have a historical span of twenty-three weeks with repeats at Christmas'.

The most sought after present on Saturday night was sex. Especially oral sex. Being expert at a 'blow-job' was regarded as a girl's best talent.

John Travolta did his research too. He visited 2001 Odyssey and found an eerie world of icemaker fog and sparkling, flashing mirrored lights. It was as if glare and subtlety had stared each other out until subtlety had withdrawn altogether.

He would visit with people from the movie and Marilu Henner, who he had linked up with (on their old platonic pals basis) following Diana Hyland's death. Brooklyn's Bay Ridge boys and girls were a new species to them.

And they were always in Travolta's thoughts. It's as though he has a videotape spinning in his head for he remembers it all: 'Meeting the kids at that 2001 Odyssey disco was a revelation to me. It's still on my mind. I think it says a lot about how we made the movie and the kids then. I went with friends and finally I did go alone. At first, because of Barbarino, I tried sort of disguises – hat, glasses. But that didn't work. So I'd go in a side entrance to a table in the back, in the shadows and it would be an hour before anybody caught sight of me.

'During those sixty minutes I concentrated like hell on every bit of those kids' behaviour that I could absorb – how they talked, little chance movements that were habit. The way they acted in the Odyssey was, like, formalised. It was a ritual with rules.

'When they recognised me they didn't yell, "Hey, it's Barbarino!" They'd say, "Hey, man! Hey, it's fucking Travolta, man!" They meant it nicely, you know?

'A guy would be talking to me, his girlfriend would approach and he'd say to her, "Get away, I'm talking to the MAN! Stay away from Travolta, don't bug him!"

'They'd actually push the girls away. Well, that wasn't in the script but I used it in the movie. They were really chauvinistic those guys.'

Especially in the back seats of cars. Why oral rather than regular sex? 'It's not a complicated thing. Maybe those guys were a little bored with so much sex available. It's kind of a novelty. But in that environment it was really a kind of birth control thing. Very important: remember the girl in the movie tells Tony she's not "protected" and he says something like, "You're not going to stick me with that problem" meaning she'll get pregnant. A lot of the kids in Brooklyn were intent on getting out. Tony Manero kind of represented them all.'

Travolta did a lot of floor training with former Locker dancer Denny Terrio, who worked with him on many of the Manero moves. He also worked with the then 18-year-old actress Fran Drescher, who was to become one of America's biggest television stars with the title role in *The Nanny*. She had a small part in *Fever* but it was a big break for her.

Travolta had said he was too tired to film a scene with her. 'I saw Travolta get cemented into his lump-like position in a corner as my part was going down the drain. I finally stomped over. "Ya know, John, maybe I shouldn't be saying this but you're a trouper. Whatever happened to 'Let's go on with the show'? So what if you're tired? So what if you're run down?

'Maybe they will have to check you into hospital for exhaustion in the end but right now I expect you to act like the star that you are and finish the scene – then we can all go home."

'I thought I'd be fired but he said, "Thanks, I needed that. Come on, let's dance." He grabbed my hand, pulled me on to the lighted disco floor and began to lead me like no man has led me before or since.'

Fran Drescher then uttered her first screen lines, 'Are you as good in bed as you are on the dance floor?'. Young, like Travolta, she improvised at that point and grabbed his backside.

Screenwriter Norman Wexler, an Oscar nominee in 1970 for *Joe* and in 1973 for *Serpico*, adapted Nik Cohn's article and created Tony Manero. Manero works in a Bay Ridge paint store and once a week gets out the disco uniform: fertility-defying gabardine trousers, floral, Brut-doused, chest-hugging shirt and platform shoes. He is the disco king. It's his older brother, a disillusioned priest played by Martin Shakar, who makes him question the parameters of his life, which are as tight as his pants.

And then, Stephanie, played by then newcomer Karen Lynn Gorney shows him a way out: the disco contest with $500 in prize money.

The three-piece polyester flared white suit which Travolta/Manero wore for the 2001 Odyssey dance contest is now in the Smithsonian Museum in Washington.

Marilu Henner was with him when Travolta found that particular piece of pop history. Along with costume designer Patrizia von Brandenstein they had searched stores in Brooklyn, Queens and Greenwich Village. It was in the Village that they found what they wanted – the suit that would stamp an image and help create a superstar.

She and Travolta had kept in contact throughout everything. Now as 'best friends' they had talked about death. She mourned the loss of her father Joe who she had watched die. He talked about Diana Hyland.

Travolta had wanted Henner to play the Stephanie role in *Fever* but Karen Lynn Gorney had won the day. This was despite Travolta's strongest efforts for his friend and former lover. He would slip Henner's photograph into John Badham's casting files. She did get an interview for the film but later revealed her 'inside' word: 'The story I heard was that I never had a shot: Badham was madly in love with Karen Lynn Gorney.'

Whatever Gorney's romantic involvements this did not stop her from feeding 'I love John' quotes to magazines and newspapers.

And it didn't stop Henner going to bat for Travolta. Years later in her autobiography she wrote, 'I got a welcome lift just being around Johnny. It was amazing to see his dream unfolding just the way we had planned it when we were starting out…'

She was around to talk when Travolta had to shoot one of the film's big scenes. Diana Hyland had only recently died and the sequence was all about the leading couple's future together or apart? Henner called it a 'poignant personal scene' for Travolta.

Tony Manero goes with Stephanie to the Verrazano Narrows Bridge, which links Brooklyn to Staten Island and on to the city and outside world. It's also the windiest place in New York City and the film crew were buffeted around as they recorded the movie's final scenes. Tony talks statistics to Stephanie: 'The towers go up 690 feet.

Centre span is 228 feet. They got forty million cars going across it a year. They got 127,000 tons of steel, almost three quarters of a million cubic yards of concrete. Centre span is 4,260 feet – total length including approach ramps – over two and a half miles'.

She hears all the anguish and hope in his voice and gives him a peck on the cheek. He doesn't respond. He avoids her eyes and he is crying. Later Travolta said that the tears had surprised him as much as they had the moviemakers. They came, maybe, from the edge of desperation

The movie's end, the ambiguous fade-out, follows. Will they be friends? Or lovers?

The original director John Avildsen wanted the couple to walk off into the sunset together but Travolta had lobbied for Norman Wexler's ending. In that version the girl, not wanting an affair, asks Manero – who is dying to have sex with her – that dauntless question, 'Can we be friends?' There is a pause and he finally says, 'Yes'. It is the mature ending, the growing up of Tony Manero.

But John Badham's ambiguity was what was filmed and it worked. It had a generation in Travolta *thralldom*.

Of course, much of the serious undertones were lost on the junior high school girls, who flipped over Travolta. 'He's a great dancer' or 'His hair is always perfect' they filled out in the preview cards. But most of all they wrote, 'He's got a great bod.'

Travolta, who wanted to be a serious actor, was suddenly The Body. He'd vetoed a 'flash' nude scene but was seen in his black briefs and that was the image that caught teenage eyes.

Like Tom Cruise's rock 'n' roll number in Ray-Bans, knickers and shirtsleeves in *Risky Business* half a dozen years later it was a pivotal career moment. Travolta later explained his motives. 'I refused to do a nude scene in *Fever* and I would still refuse. I think that you should put just enough out there to get people excited – but not too much. Women are very aggressive about what they want. They lay it right on the line. It's not romantic, innocent passion they want to tell you about nowadays…'

Nevertheless the new star had insisted, 'I like being a sex symbol but I'm being appraised more as an actor than a sex symbol.'

The language in *Fever* was strong, and so were the teenage sex scenes in the back of cars. One guy is with a girl and asks her, 'What did you say your name was?' The sleaze laughs and the language brought criticism of Travolta. He thought the film, not the criticism, serious.

'My fans will have to grow with me. I don't want to be considered a teen idol for the rest of my life,' was his response.

The critics were impressed with Travolta the actor. There was one scene where Tony stops off for a snack and orders pizza, two slices, and in a Travolta moment piles them on top of each other and munches. His sister had her one line in the film

Cool – 1978 style. Travolta in *that* white suit in his legendary role as disco king Tony Manero in *Saturday Night Fever*.

You're the one that I want…
the first screen coupling of
Travolta and Olivia Newton-
John; the leader of the
Grease gang.

In the driving seat: the breakthrough role for Travolta with Nancy Allen in Brian De Palma's *Carrie*.

An affair to forget: Travolta and *Moment by Moment* screen lover Lily Tomlin. The movie doesn't appear in his personal filmography.·

Pleased to see me? Travolta and *Urban Cowboy* co-star Debra Winger go hat-to-hat.

Mirror image: Travolta reunited with Nancy Allen and director Brian De Palma in what many regard as his best dramatic role in *Blow Out*.

Still *Staying Alive* in 1983 but there was much toil and trouble getting into shape for director Sylvester Stallone.

Look who's twisting?
Baby talk from
parents Travolta and
Kelly Preston and
superstar couple
Demi Moore and
Bruce Willis.

MA DE ORO — FESTIVAL CANNES 1994 · PULP FICTION · un film de Quentin Tarantino

Happy poster boys: Bruce Willis and Travolta in the Quentin Tarantino movie that brought him back to life.

The tuxedo matches: Travolta with wife Kelly Preston at the 1996 'Golden Globe Awards' in Beverly Hills.

Travolta as the suddenly super-smart George Malley with Robert Duvall as 'Doc' in 1996's *Phenomenon*.

Gangster rap: author Douglas Thompson flanked by Travolta and Samuel L. Jackson in *Pulp Fiction* pose.

in that scene, 'How many slices?' His mother also appeared, as a customer in the paint store where Tony worked. Family *Fever* which, of course, was a sensation.

With one hand stabbing at the sky and the Persil-white suit blazing Travolta *was* Tony Manero the Disco King. He was no longer Fred Kelly's pupil – he was Gene Kelly's potential movie replacement.

The film's not so secret weapon was the soundtrack, with songs from the Bee Gees recorded at the Chateau d'Herouville studios (Elton John had put it on the map with his 1972 *Honky Chateau* album) outside Paris. The group had planned to record their follow-up to *Children of the World* there but Stigwood had asked for new songs for a film.

'We never saw any script,' said Barry Gibb. 'We were told it was about a bunch of guys that live in New York.' Later, Stigwood gave them a better outline. 'And we knew John Travolta was playing the part.'

'How Deep Is Your Love' was the first soundtrack single issued before the movie opened in America on 12 December 1977 making it eligible for that year's Academy Awards set to be presented in April 1978. The single was in the Top Ten for seventeen weeks, the longest run of any single since the charts began and was followed by 'Stayin' Alive', 'Night Fever' and 'More Than A Woman' which became disco and the movie's anthems.

Seven days before *Fever* hit cinemas a 30-second trailer of the opening sequence, with the pounding 'Stayin' Alive' playing was seen all over America. The demand for the movie and the song were overwhelming.

The soundtrack sold more than twenty-five million copies and was the bestselling LP ever, until 1984 when another dancing whiz called Michael Jackson broke its record with *Beat It*.

John Travolta, acting, singing, dancing, was on top of the world. *Fever* had earned more than $81 million in its first sixteen weeks in America alone: eleven times the break-even figure.

Many years later Travolta would recall all the hysteria, the première parties in New York and Hollywood, the glitz and the glamour. And the beginnings of fame in which nobody is giving and they all want something from you. 'I remember saying to myself, "How do you top this?" Even if you do, it can only happen to you once because you're only surprised once. You're forced to compete with yourself and you're maxed out. So you just do good work and hope you can stay there.'

Then, it seemed, he would stay alive forever. And in a way, in that mirrored light and white suit as Tony Manero, he was immortal.

By January 1978 the Hollywood Foreign Press had gathered at the Beverly Hills Hilton Hotel to announce that he was a nominee for a Golden Globe as Best Actor.

His cross-section of fans was widening: teeny-boppers, feverish women, and the gay disco crowd which brought whispers about Travolta's own sexuality, the first of the gay rumours that were to haunt his career. Even as his Golden Globe nomination was announced he had to attend to that issue: 'Fame is very exciting. I take it for what it is – admiration. I don't know about the gay reaction. I would imagine there is appeal there too. But the observer views my success more drastically than I do.'

At the same time he was talking to the trustees of the Ahmanson Centre in Los Angeles about putting on his own production of Tennessee Williams' *Sweet Bird of Youth*. Everybody wanted him. He was the 'new' Rudolph Valentino. But half a century earlier H. L. Mencken had written, 'In brief, Valentino's agony was the agony of man of relatively civilised feelings thrown into a situation of intolerable vulgarity, destructive alike to his peace and to his dignity.'

Supply and demand, dignity and box office: as one went up the other seemed to go down. Bob Le Mond and Lois Zetter were proving themselves gems at guiding Travolta over the hurdles. He was Travolta – not Barbarino or Tony Manero.

Travolta was still – by contract – Vinnie Barbarino, but the prospect of him returning to *Kotter* after *Fever* was like Garbo joining *Charlie's Angels* to replace the then Farrah Fawcett-Majors. From January to March 1978, the movie was earning $600,000 a day.

The world – particularly Paramount Pictures – was Travolta-happy. When it appeared that a rival company were going to star Joey Travolta in a television disco series, Paramount jumped in and hired him on $50,000 a year. Ellen Travolta had more work than she could handle. Bob Le Mond and Lois Zetter were made 'producers' to 'develop film and TV projects' for Paramount.

'If their presence on the Paramount lot results in John Travolta agreeing to do one small film then Paramount will come out ahead,' was the view of observer Dwight Whitney.

Over at the ABC television network the affable and talented Tony Thomopoulos had taken over in February 1978, as president of the company's entertainment division and had to cope with the issue of whether or not Travolta would stay with Kotter.

He explained to a clutch of TV writers at the time, 'After I took the job I had a meeting with John Travolta and his agents. As you all know, John is the equivalent of Paul Newman, Steve McQueen and Robert Redford thanks to his phenomenal success in *Saturday Night Fever* .

'John started off telling me, "I have an obligation to perform in twenty two episodes of *Welcome Back, Kotter* this coming season. I believe in keeping my word.

However, you can understand that there are other calls on my time. Still, I intend to honour my obligation." We talked about it and we happily came to the decision that John will star in eight episodes of *Kotter* for us. His attitude was marvellous and I applaud Mr Travolta.'

Part of the deal also included a Scientology auditor being on the set of *Kotter* whenever Travolta was working. He wanted to be 'calm' – but the offers were pouring in from all over the world.

'Is there any film with a male lead between fourteen and 60 where they are not discussing John Travolta?' Bob Le Mond understandably gloated in a major magazine article.

His client was thinking, thinking, thinking. He had devoted himself to Tony Manero but said, 'Even when I saw all Tony's levels he still didn't seem to me a sympathetic character.

'He's really mean to women. He's so angry. I finally figured that I had to incorporate into him a strong line of integrity.

'He finds a girl he looks up to and sticks with her even though she's a bitch and he sticks with her dream which is also his. That gets you right back to what I observed about the actual guys on the Brooklyn streets: a rough kind of integrity.

'They have standards. To try to find Tony's appealingness that fact was the source.'

John Travolta was now legally a corporation and convinced that his strength came from Scientology. Although it was derided and feared by many, he felt that it was a way to help himself find answers in his life.

By now he had built up – so far mostly on the telephone – a strong rapport with Olivia Newton-John who was to co-star with him in *Grease*. He had also bought a 23-seat DC3 plane instead of a house. His mother thought it was as big as some of the homes in their New Jersey neighbourhood. And more luxurious.

But there wasn't anything to fly away from.

Was there?

Chapter Twelve
The One They Want

'After the kiss comes the impulse to throttle.' W. H. Auden

The *great* surprise of 1978, with hindsight, is that John Travolta did not simply fly out of the world. He had excuses for going but what kept him on the ground was his success. The dream – of his mother, his family, friends and Diana Hyland – was happening.

He was a movie star and Bob Le Mond, as ever, was his guide. Lois Zetter recalls him telling her, 'John is surrounded by people who are totally committed to him as a talent – and as a human being.'

The inner circle certainly were. And Travolta inspired others to try to protect him. Le Mond recalled, during the *Fever* filming: 'Even the chauffeur wanted to work seven days a week because on Saturdays he worried that other drivers were not taking care of John.'

Everyone on the film was actually taking care of business. But Travolta, typically, was taking care of the family. He moved his parents from Englewood – all the children had long gone by then – to Los Angeles where they settled happily but with bemusement into a Hollywood lifestyle. There were trips to Hawaii with Sam and Helen sitting up front in First Class with luaus around their necks and Irish coffees in their hands.

They travelled with him on film promotions where he became a little kid again going, 'Look Mom! Look Dad!' The difference this time was that he was picking up the bills. The bigger they were for his parents the happier he was. In Britain Sam Travolta balked at the price of his favourite cigars but his son tipped the hotel's night manager to ensure that boxes of them were always in his father's room. Then he checked with his mother to make sure his father was smoking them.

Helen Travolta was as frugal as her husband, splitting breakfasts with him in the South of France. 'Think of this money like Monopoly – the studio's paying,' he would tell them. Travolta would sit and watch his mother eat. Her appetite wasn't great and he'd say, 'Spoil yourself a little, Ma.' Helen told a friend, 'We'd have been happier in a second-class hotel. That's where people like us belong but that would have hurt Johnny's feelings. Johnny deserves all the fuss. I haven't done anything to deserve this.'

From Europe it was first class back to California.

Olivia Newton-John's dreams were also soaring. Her big night had been at the Metropolitan Opera House in New York in 1977. Like the Bee Gees, she had been born in Britain and raised in Australia. The line about her was that if white bread could sing it would sound just like Olivia Newton-John.

Her appeal had crossed over from pop into country and back again. When casting was going on for *Grease* in 1977 she had been in America for five years and had collected six platinum albums (two double platinum), seven gold singles including 'Honestly Love You' and 'Have You Ever Been Mellow', three Grammys and a roomful of other music and entertainer awards.

Still, she was nervous sitting in her suite at the Sherry Netherlands Hotel in New York, playing the Broadway cast album of *Grease*. She'd had a stereo system installed so that she could play and play the music.

What matters at a Hollywood dinner party is not the meal but the deal. Australian singer Helen Reddy and her then husband and manager Jeff Wald were experts at entertaining at home. She was trying to find a girl for Californian Governor ('Governor Moonbeam') Jerry Brown to ease him out of his relationship with singer Linda Ronstadt. He was late and they started dinner without him. The focus was on another guest: Allan Carr. He had signed John Travolta for *Grease* but he needed a leading lady. He mentioned names: Ann-Margret, Marie Osmond, Susan Dey (*The Partridge Family* actress who graduated to *L.A. Law*). Then he looked across the table into the blue eyes of Reddy's friend Olivia Newton-John. A deal was done. It was a tough one.

Newton-John, in her movie debut, would get equal billing with Travolta. The pay was a boot sale $125,000. The director would be Randal Kleiser who had been so helpful to Travolta in *The Boy in the Plastic Bubble*.

She had made one film – the silly nonsense *Tomorrow* in 1970, which was created around a contrived pop group like The Monkees – but this would be her first major film appearance. She was to play Sandy, the goody-goody love of Travolta's Danny Zuko, the tearaway teddy-boy with slicked-down attitude and duck-tail hairstyle. Danny meets and falls for Aussie import Sandy – to cover Newton-John's Down Under twang – on a seaside holiday, but back at Rydell High School he is the leader of the pack – of high-school wolves. This was the dawning of the age of electric guitars, and fluorescent socks were an indication of independence. It was 50s rock 'n' roll, 'You Ain't Nothing But A Hound Dog' and

'Blue Suede Shoes'. It was all teenage jiving, jitterbugging and groping.

Sandy gets her man by switching from summer frock to skintight pants and leather jacket, turning herself into a gum-cracking biker moll. Newton-John didn't know if her fans would accept that. 'I wasn't too happy – I didn't want to go into something I couldn't handle or have something to say about. I was mixed-up and frightened. I kept thinking, "Here am I a singer wanting to be an actress working with an actor who sings." '

At 29 she was playing a character a dozen years her junior. She was not bashful about asking for script changes and a screen test. 'I was playing a naive girl but I didn't want her to be sickly. I kept trying to give her a little strength.'

After Vinnie Barberino and Tony Manero, her co-star faced a similar dilemma: would his fans go for a softer character? He wanted to move on from *Kotter* and *Fever* and 'develop'. But he was there to help the newcomer. 'John gave me a lot of confidence. We became good friends and spent a lot of time together.'

It seemed like a coupling made in publicity and personal heaven. Through tragedy Travolta was available and Newton-John had separated from her manager/lover Lee Kramer when they began filming. Gossip columnists filled space and the entertainment magazines ran linking articles. On television in the embryo days of American TV gossip they were not only upbeat to talk about, they made good pictures too.

Friends say they became lovers and it is difficult to imagine them not being, but both have always skirted the issue. They did, however, become solid friends and remained so through the 1980s and 1990s.

Years after the dinner party at Helen Reddy's, Newton-John put the home she had had custom built in the hills above Pacific Cove in Malibu on the market. With an asking price of $7.5 million dollars, at 48 she said she was 'scaling down' and first to go, was that sprawling horse ranch home. The same month *It's My Party*, a film written and directed by Randal Kleiser – and based on his best friend's death from AIDS – opened in America. Newton-John played a friend of Eric Roberts' dying architect and sang 'Don't Cut Me Down' during the film's closing credits.

She, like Travolta, had bounced back from much adversity. And their battles with life kept them closer through the years. She and Matt Lattanzi, her husband, were one of Travolta's adopted 'families', there to support him when he needed it.

Before she sold her home, she sat on her patio and talked about early Travolta and the runaway success of the movie: 'I didn't care what the critics said, I was thrilled with it. I was extremely lucky to be in a film with John. He's a great actor. He has incredible charisma, great sensitivity and a great presence on screen. Everything comes from inside; it comes out more on the screen than when you're actually working beside him.

'When I was offered the part in *Grease* John wasn't yet a star but I had heard that he was going to be. We hit it off really well together. He was very gentle, sensitive, funny, very professional.

'I had no acting training when I started *Grease*. Most of my acting was completely instinctive, I just went into it the way I felt it should be. If something was wrong John would help me in every way.

'Once we were doing this scene where we met again at school. It was a reaction shot – John was off-camera. Halfway through the shot John made a mistake so we had to start all over again.

'Later he told me that he had thought I could do the whole scene better so he deliberately made that mistake. I thought that was very generous. There aren't many people who would do that for someone else.'

Travolta helped her again – in Las Vegas. He was in the audience watching one of her shows when he leaped up on stage and sang and danced a *Grease* number with her. She remembered:

'The audience went wild. It was a wonderful night. I didn't think my career could get any better but after *Grease* it's soared and soared. I was a little wary of making a film because I had made one before and it was a bad experience.

'*Tomorrow* was about a pop group who got taken up into outer space. They were trying to make us into The Monkees of the 70s. It was awful — it opened and closed in about a week.' In contrast *Grease* goes on and on.

She prepared for her role by recalling her lonely days as an 'outcast' at school in Britain. 'I tried to remember back to when I was 17 — that's a long time ago now! — and how a girl felt in the 50s to be in a completely new environment. It wasn't so difficult for me because when I was young we left England for Australia and when I came back I had an Australian accent. I know what it feels like to be an outsider... The only one with a funny accent.

'I came to Hollywood originally because I had a hit record in Australia and I came over to promote it. Then I had another hit record and on my second trip I ran into Helen Reddy and she told me, "If you're really going to make it in America you'll have to stay here. You can't do it half-heartedly." I thought about it. I knew I had a chance for great success here so I took Helen's advice and took the gamble.'

Ironically she became a a greater success in America than her close friend Cliff Richard, who helped to start her career in Britain and who had tried to branch out to America in 1976. 'I seem to have known Cliff forever. He and John Travolta were wonderful to me, always genuine and helpful. They were real stars.

'I started singing when I was 15 and still in Australia. In the beginning I didn't have any great ambition, I was just enjoying it. Then I went back to England and joined up with another girl and we did a double act touring the Army bases and singing in clubs for very little money.

'But it was all great fun. When I became a solo artist I was very lucky because there have always been people behind me who believed in me and what I was doing. That encouraged me to keep going.

'I always believe in fate – what was meant to happen was going to happen, you couldn't force it. When I look back now I was working in some pretty awful places – singing to waiters and barmen – but it was all experience I had to gain.'

But it was not enough to win the role she had coveted since *Grease* days – that of Evita. As Madonna was making the role her own, opposite Jonathan Pryce's Peron, Newton-John was settling Down Under. Even then she and Travolta enjoyed long phone conversations. He felt for her: at almost the same age as Diana Hyland she had become a victim of breast cancer.

She found out about it in 1992 and everything changed; her marriage, her attitudes, her ambitions. For the first time she found the confidence to write a whole album of highly personal songs of her own, *Gaia: One Woman's Journey*, and she was forced to reassess herself through regular sessions with a psychiatrist.

'I started being able to express feelings I thought I shouldn't have. I learned to express anger, to shout and bang doors, which I always found very hard before. I learned not to feel guilty all the time about being so successful. I used to feel undeserving about having things handed to me on a platter when people around me didn't.

'I know I used to be a kind of victim in that I allowed things to happen rather than taking control. I'd give in, when I didn't really want to do something. It would often be little things like wanting to be alone but not saying so, or going somewhere when I was really tired.

'I was trying to do the right thing all the time, lest people thought I was too selfish. And there was just too much of that. I wouldn't speak up. I was a very fearful person, and probably too scared to think deeply about myself. I didn't have time to reflect until I got sick. But having cancer has freed me and helped me grow up. It has, in retrospect, been a very positive experience.'

She first suspected that something was wrong when she began too feel uncharacteristically listless. Six months later, she discovered a lump in one of her breasts. A mammogram proved negative as did a biopsy. To be absolutely certain she underwent a lumpectomy.

Afterwards, she put it out of her mind and flew off with husband Matt Lattanzi for a Fourth of July weekend. But just before take-off there was a phone call for him at the airport. The news was bad. Her father, a retired college dean, had just died of liver cancer and her doctor in Los Angeles needed to see her again. Urgently.

Matt told her about her father's death later that evening, but said nothing about the doctor's message. 'I have always loved him for that. I was in such pain over my father, and Matt knew it was enough for me to deal with.'

The following Monday, her doctor told her she had cancer. 'My way of coping with it was to crack jokes. I thought: "What else can go wrong?" I laughed a lot.'

Later, it hit her: 'I woke up in the middle of the night and went downstairs. Then I just felt terror down to my boots. My knees and legs went weak and I thought the cancer must have spread right through my body.'

As far as possible she was relentlessly positive. She remembers signing a consent form for a double mastectomy, should it be found necessary, and making light of it all as she was prepared for surgery. 'I didn't want to upset the people around me.'

She sounded like Diana Hyland and, after talking to other women with breast cancer, she believed she was probably quite a typical victim.

'Most of us are a certain type who don't know how to express ourselves. We try to be everything to everybody, we give, we don't take care of ourselves emotionally. We do things for everybody else and repress our own desires and feelings.' She believes the pattern was probably set in childhood.

Her father had never been able to express emotions either, even during the week she spent with him just before he died. 'The closest he came then was by reading out some poems to my sister and me; he was trying to say something through poetry because he couldn't express himself. I loved him very much but he was not a person who spoke about his feelings, so I don't feel I really knew the real him underneath.'

Her parents had separated when she was ten. 'I don't think I had a happy childhood. My parents' divorce made me feel insecure. I tried to blank out what was going on, and I was always the "happy" child trying to keep everyone else happy.'

At 15, she won a singing contest, with the prize of a year in Britain which her mother eagerly accepted on her behalf. But she was madly in love with her boyfriend and determined not to leave:

'I was still underage, so my mother tore me away from him and kind of dragged me to England by my ear. When I got there I kept booking return tickets to Australia but she would find out and cancel them. I even ran to a lawyer to see if I could be made a ward of court. I was in love and my hormones were going crazy. But my mother thought I was too young for romance. She was right, of course.

'I was quite naive then and although people were doing drugs around me I never seemed to notice. I floated through on this little cloud of everything being lovely. I'd have done better to play against my looks, maybe shaved my head and worn grungy clothes. But that's just not how I was; even my music was pretty wholesome.'

It was a similar image she took to America and *Grease*. There were a couple of long relationships, including the one with Lee Kramer, but both fizzled out. 'I was terrified of marriage,' she admits. Almost her entire family had gone through divorces and she had no intention of following them.

'If you've never seen a relationship that lasts you tend to believe it's not possible. I think people give up on marriage too easily. It's worth working through the hard times, getting through to the other side and finding it was worth hanging on. My own view is that six months of counselling should be part of the divorce process. 'I've been to counselling and Matt has been involved, too. No marriage is without problems.'

And there were problems.

She met Matt Lattanzi, an actor eleven years younger than herself, when she filmed *Xanadu* with Gene Kelly in 1980. 'I was paranoid about the age difference at first. Younger men with older women weren't so common then, and of course I always wanted to do the right thing.'

They married in 1984. He seemed a good bet, she says, because he came from a family of nine in which there is only one divorce to date. The birth of their daughter Chloe in 1986 was followed by three miscarriages, one at nearly five months. ('I grieved for them all'.) Her sports-clothing empire, Koala Blue, crashed amid debts and recriminations. Her husband's career faltered.

Her cancer surgery involved a partial mastectomy and she had her breast reconstructed at the same time. Then she went through eight months of chemotherapy supplemented by homeopathy.

There were many times, she says, when she thought she would die if she fell asleep. 'I felt constantly nauseous, headachy, sleepy. I was in a fog, and my short–term memory, which can be affected by chemotherapy, became terrible.'

When the treatment ended she and Matt moved to New South Wales for six months where she owns a 200-acre avocado farm on the edge of a rainforest. She enjoyed the solitude until her husband had a nervous breakdown. 'He would shake, cry uncontrollably and scream into his pillow.'

It took three months for him to recover. 'I hadn't been aware of his fear and I don't think even he was aware of it at the time. It's very difficult for the people around you sometimes. They try to hold you up, but it's frightening for them. Matt suffered from a kind of delayed shock.'

She maintained in 1996 that her marriage was 'fine' but she also pointed out, 'I think cancer changes a relationship. It has to. It puts stress on it but it also makes the relationship more honest.'

Newton-John's disease had rattled her: 'I'm not ambitious in the same way any more. I feel anything I achieve from now on is a blessing. You're never pronounced cured with cancer, though they say with each year, your chances get better. As far as I'm concerned I *am* cured. Mental attitude is a great part of staying healthy so I need to believe that. I simply must.'

She was a positive supporter for Travolta, sending him telegrams and taking out a big advertisement in the trade paper the *Hollywood Reporter* in March 1996, to mark his selection as ShoWest Male Star of the Year. The advertisement read: *'Dear Danny, I am "Hopelessly Devoted To You".*' It was signed *'Love, Sandy.'*

Travolta was delighted. As he was with similar advertisements taken out by Tom Cruise and Nicole Kidman and the Church of Scientology Celebrity Centre International on Hollywood's Franklin Avenue.

In 1978 Olivia Newton-John's home was in Malibu's Big Rock Canyon. There were telephones in the bathrooms! Travolta was then living in his spartan one-bedroom apartment at 100 South Doheny in Beverly Hills down from Sunset Boulevard and above Santa Monica Boulevard. He had been to Europe, on ski trips to California's Mammoth Mountain a five-hour drive from Los Angeles but he wasn't yet a sophisticate. At the Oscar ceremonies that year, he was nominated as Best Actor and he had plenty of competition: Richard Burton for *Equus*, Marcello Mastroianni for *A Special Day*, Woody Allen for *Annie Hall* and, the eventual winner, Richard Dreyfuss for *The Goodbye Girl.*

Dreyfuss was the antithesis of Travolta. He was a real life graduate from Beverly Hills High School – and the television antics of the 1990s *Beverly Hills 90210* kids were nothing on the real thing – and ran his fame in the fast lane, all cognac and cocaine, until he gave it all up in the 1980s.

Travolta wasn't just from the other side of the tracks he was from the other side of the country but on Oscars night they got on. They were both from strongly bonded families.

Sam and Helen Travolta were at the Dorothy Chandler Pavilion with their son. He and the family felt he was the outsider; that itself, of course, gave hope, for the underdog winning is all part of the American Dream. Later, Helen would tell of how Richard Burton had come over to them and joked to her son, 'If you take it from me big boy I'll bust your beautiful chops.'

As always the ceremonies were long and Travolta's mother was uncomfortable. He spent the evening – more than five hours – massaging her numb knees. He smiled at the cameras but was frowning inside. He offered to take her home, but she refused to budge. They would have to carry her out of there! Her son might win an Oscar at any moment.

Helen Travolta's discomfort was an early sign of the cancer that would kill her later that year. In December – the same month as his mother's death – he heard the phrase 'your career is over' for the first time. Yet he was also being presented with a string of offers. It is an indication of the time it can take to get a movie made in Hollywood that they included *Interview With A Vampire*, which was finally filmed with Tom Cruise in 1994, and *Godfather III*, which became the breakthrough movie for Andy Garcia in 1991. Garcia played the surrogate son of Al Pacino's Michael Corleone – the role planned all those years earlier for Travolta.

It's confusing when you are the only one they want and a moment later it all changes. In this case, as he and Olivia Newton-John soared in the biggest box-office musical ever, the change came with *Moment by Moment*.

Chapter Thirteen
Catch a Falling Star

'You see him, you fall in love with him a little bit.'

Lily Tomlin on co-star John Travolta, 1978

*G**rease* was a sensation worldwide. If Travolta had been hot before, he was now off the thermometer. Everything and everyone connected with the movie took off and the boulevards were alive with the sound of 'yes' men.

'He is the street Tyrone Power,' pronounced Allan Carr. Travolta put himself in the league of Mr Method, telling the austere *Time* magazine, 'I'd decided not to do the part but then I reconsidered. I thought: "What's wrong with doing a light musical? Brando did it." '

The magic formula, the one everyone seeks but no one writes down, worked. The greatest hit songs were all written for the film and the Travolta/Newton-John 'You're The One That I Want' was the first single released. As *Grease* opened so did the song, at 65 in the American Hot Hundred. Ten weeks later it was number one.

In Britain it was number one for nine weeks, tying as the single to stay longest in the charts with Paul Anka's 'Diana' in 1957. 'Summer Nights' from the stage show was number five in America but in the UK they loved the Hollywood couple and it stayed at number one for seven weeks.

Travolta was in a spin. Stockard Channing, who played Rizzo, the leader of the Pink Ladies in *Grease*, says the film remains with all involved with it. In 1996 she was starring as Harvey Keitel's lover in director Wayne Wang's *Smoke* but admitted, 'People still ask me about Rizzo and *Grease*. It was a job. I needed the money but it was a romp. I never realised it would turn into this phenomenon over years and years and years.

'Who knew? To be standing on the steps of a high school and burst into song was pretty much a fantasy all of us had. Then, John Travolta was part of a hurricane. He'd just got an Academy Award nomination. He was pretty young and he'd just had a personal tragedy in that the woman he loved had died from cancer. He was pretty shell-shocked.

'I remember I liked him very much. He was kind of in a spin cycle which is understandable. But he had then – which he still seems to have – that kind of grace and balance.'

Travolta was trying to balance his emotional life. He was about to film *Moment by Moment* with Lily Tomlin. British actress Kate Edwards, who worked with him as director of development of Travolta Productions from 1978 to 1982 and dated him, reflected in 1996, 'When he plays a character who struggles to treat a woman as a woman and not just as a sex object audiences love him. When you combine the story element with great music which enhances John's innate body language then you have the recipe for what makes him a trendsetter.'

Trendsetting was not what they said about *Moment by Moment.* It was the last part of his contract hat-trick with Robert Stigwood. Lily Tomlin – then best known as Ernestine the telephonist in television's *Laugh-In* – and he were swiftly involved in a mutual admiration pact. 'We are very much in tune. We feel like we knew each other in another time,' he announced.

Travolta played Strip, a delivery boy who meets a bored, wealthy Malibu housewife who seduces him. But – cue heavenly music – it turns into love. Then, Travolta said: 'I play a more sensitive role. I'm not just an uncouth lad with lots of sex appeal but not much else. In this film a relationship develops.'

Much was made of the similarities between this screen partnership and his own with Diana Hyland. And he said he identified with the situation: 'I felt strongly for Strip. Part of him was in me. Beneath the street macho he has a genuine honesty and truthfulness. I think I've experienced what he does in the story. It's not exactly the same, the character is more innocent than I am, although I was once like him. I think it's about time men were shown to have feelings and be tender. I feel that way in my private life.'

It was a life that the Hollywood gossips wanted to know and write about. Marilu Henner's name constantly bubbled up (they were still 'just friends') and as well as Olivia Newton-John there were Marisa Berenson – then, at 31, a perfect media 'older woman' – and Priscilla Presley, then 33, with whom he shared a Scientology connection. It was like picking names from a hat and the gossips were as likely to get a white rabbit as Liza Minnelli or Streisand. Cher, just separated from rock-star husband Gregg Allman, was a serious contender and they had several dinner dates at her Hollywood Hills home. Sam Travolta was amused at his son's love life: 'They've always got him with some girl or other.'

But despite the fluttering females all around him, Travolta said, 'One-nighters are more exciting to think about than they are in reality. At least, that's been my experience.'

Privately, he said he still felt 'helpless' following Diana Hyland's death. He felt most comfortable with Kate Edwards and the fact that her mother Joan, who worked for him as an assistant, went with them on trips eased any heavy pressure. The memories came back, however, when he accompanied Diana's parents at their request to accept her posthumous Emmy – the 'TV Oscar' – for her work in *Eight Is Enough*. He waved the statuette in the air and said: 'Here's to you, Diana, wherever you are!'. (Later, he said, 'It was a painful moment. I'm strong, though. I've always been a fighter.')

At the same time Joan Prather, who had introduced him to Scientology, was getting married to Scientology minister James Fiducia. Asked about his bride's past love, the groom replied, 'I've never been jealous of my beautiful wife going with John.' Prather gushed, 'I'll always love Johnny and I think Johnny will always be in love with me to a certain extent. He seemed quite shocked when I told him I was getting married. But we still went out a few times.' When asked about this her husband said, 'It would bother me if I couldn't let her do what she wants to do.'

On the surface it appeared that Travolta could do anything *he* wanted. But could he? He had learned the limitations of stardom at the start of *Welcome Back, Kotter* and recalled, 'They treated us all like dumb kids and the more famous we got and the more valuable we got to the moneymen the more like kids they treated us. People are so desperate to be in control – to be powerful – that they want to conquer you.'

On *Moment by Moment* he felt conquered-out. He said later that he knew the movie would fail. He had wanted to quit during filming but Bob Le Mond – probably wisely – advised him against it. 'He said I'd get a bad rep if I left, that it was too early in my career for me to call the shots. So I hung on. It was torture.'

But not half as bad as when the critics shredded the movie. He was expecting the onslaught but says it still shocked him. 'It put me away for a while – I mean it just *hurt* me. But later I could handle it. Most people don't see it anyway.'

It was following the completion of *Moment by Moment* that his world collapsed. His mother had been ailing and the family had tried to keep the seriousness of her illness from him. But she became more frail.

Then his father suffered a heart-attack. It was serious and scared the whole family, but he slowly recovered. It was the only good news.

By then Helen's cancer was pronounced terminal. 'For John his mom was the most important woman in the world,' said family friend Peggy O'Boyle. 'Helen always bragged about what a wonderful boy he was. She never called him anything but "my baby". '

In November 1978, her left breast was removed after the discovery of a malignant lump but the surgery did not stop the spread of cancer. Although he now knew she was dying, Travolta did not realise how swiftly his mother would succumb. He planned to take her as his 'date' to the Hollywood première of *Moment by Moment* on 22 December. 'John had gotten her a gorgeous outfit to wear at the opening. He wanted her to go there like a queen,' recalled Beatrice Wides, one of his mother's best friends.

Travolta himself recalled earlier, reluctant shopping trips with his mother. 'After I got rich I took her to Bergdorf's department store in New York. She kept looking at price tags when she thought I wasn't watching her and she wouldn't buy a thing. She never got used to having money in the family. She never believed it belonged to her by right. And she was sick then – dying – and thinking it was wrong to spend my money...'

He spent hours with Helen in her room in the white-painted West Tower of Cedars-Sinai Medical Centre off San Vicente Boulevard in Hollywood. 'He wanted to make it easier for her to pass on,' remembered Joan Prather.

Travolta also wanted his mother to go with dignity. He had suffered what he felt was intrusive press during Diana Hyland's final moments and at her cremation and burial service. He was working on *Kotter* the day his mother died, aged 66 on 3 December 1978, but no one knew of his personal grief. The *Los Angeles Times*, the *Los Angeles Herald-Examiner* and the Hollywood trade papers missed the event.

It allowed him and twenty-nine other mourners, all family and close friends, to attend the ceremony in peace at Forest Lawn Cemetery in Los Angeles. Travolta arranged for his mother's friend, the Rev Odilardo Arceo, to conduct the funeral service at the cemetery where Valentino and Marilyn Monroe are buried. He stood, head bowed, beside the open grave, which was surrounded by bouquets of his mother's favourite flowers.

The next day he was back at work on *Kotter*. Marcia Strassman tried to comfort him. 'You know, John had two deaths in the time we were doing *Kotter* and these were the only two times I'd seen Johnny upset. He'd just get real quiet, very quiet. I mean if you know him really well his face is an open book.'

She gave a keen insight into Travolta's relationship with his mother and her relationship with him. 'She would have killed for him and when you love someone that much it's always someone you have problems with. She wanted him to be a success so much. I'm sure that was a problem for him for a long time but he adored her.

'And when *Saturday Night Fever* happened it was like, Helen took a deep breath and said, "Okay, I can die happy – I've seen him get what he deserves." When his mom died everything just sort of sagged. He could finally admit he was tired and just say, "I can't". It's very hard for Johnny to say "I can't" about anything.'

His co-star Ron Palillo said, 'I am sure it was a strain for him getting back on the show. We had made every effort to ease John's pain while his mother was dying and we did the same after she had passed on. But it was tough for everybody.'

And it was tougher on him than anyone really knew. A truly bad sleeper, he was not even getting the rest he usually managed.

He had just won the lead in *American Gigolo* and Paramount Studios had an education planned for him. Hollywood sophisticate Francis Lederer was to tutor him in urbane graces (for a graceful fee of $500 a day) while he was sent to Milan to be dressed to ladykill in fine Armani fashions (when the movie was finally made and reviewed, some critics said the clothes were the stars). He was one day away from learning his lines when he realised he could not go through with the movie.

Moment by Moment had been hung, drawn and quartered. He had endured his terrible family tragedies and this was given as the reason he walked out on *Gigolo*. But Travolta said:

'I tell you honestly I was thinking all the time of the pizzazz of the film, of the body language – I wasn't seeing that the dialogue was stilted. Then I met the writer-director Paul Schrader and he was so rigid about his words on the page, so possessive of his words…the more meetings I had with him the more uncomfortable I became. One night – I remember exactly where it was, in the kitchen of my house – I turned to my assistant Kay and said, "I have a nauseous feeling in my stomach. I shouldn't be doing this, should I?" Kay said: "No." The next day I told the producers I was out.'

His co-star, supermodel/actress/adventuress Lauren Hutton, was in a remote area of Mexico. Paramount were in a tizzy. Travolta's then press agent Michelle Cohen issued a statement: 'John has been through so much this year. This is common sense. He did *Saturday Night Fever*, *Grease* and *Moment by Moment* without a break and was also taping *Welcome Back, Kotter*. He is going to take a long rest.'

Travolta sacrificed $1.5 million and got a reputation around town for being 'difficult'. Paramount's diplomatic press release, which said that Travolta was pulling out because of his mother's death and father's illness was pre-empted by Jack Martin, who broke the story in the *New York Post*.

Hollywood hammered away at Travolta, not knowing that it had been his doubts about the film rather than simply his mother's death and the *Moment by Moment* fiasco that had made him walk away. (The role eventually went to Richard Gere, who also had reservations about it related to his Buddhist beliefs.)

James Bacon, a legend in print and his own lunchtime, wrote, 'John Travolta is one very unhappy movie star. He's gotten very depressed over his experience. This has recently sent him into a blue funk.'

There was much similar stuff but Helen Travolta's younger sister Mildred said,

'It was absolute nonsense. His mother's death hit him harder than any other member of the family. And he was worried about my brother-in-law's health. It took him a long time to accept his mother's death – a small part of him refused to believe it. He was always like that. He thought he could change bad things.

'My husband John and I had had no kids of our own so it was natural we devoted ourselves to Sam and Helen's children. We live near them in Hillsdale. We were like second parents to them. Young John was born on my husband's birthday. That's how he got the name John. I'm still his second mother but I could never have replaced Helen.

'After his mother died he did everything he could to help his father despite the hurt he was feeling inside. He did everything he could to get Sam over the death of Helen. He took him on trips. They went partying together – anything John could do for his father he did. Of course, he was helping himself as well but he did it mainly for his father. '

Critics, however, were everywhere. The East German youth newspaper *Junge Welt* said, 'Travolta tries to make capitalistic daily life seem harmless'. In Moscow, *Pravda* decided, 'He is really washed-up. Only one joy is left to him – the childish habit of gluing together brightly-painted model airplanes.'

One of the kinder reviews of *Moment by Moment* asked: 'Is this someone's idea of a big joke?' Another saw Travolta as 'served-up as a kind of hairy-chested Jane Russell – a bimbo'.

Travolta decided to buy a house – with an aircraft landing strip. That way he could take off anytime he wanted.

Bob Le Mond was, as always, there for him: 'For four years John was on a skyrocket. He had not had time to deal with the deaths, to adjust to his change in financial status or to accept the criticism of *Moment*. He was physically exhausted.'

Travolta himself recalled those mad days: 'The whole thing was so crazy. When all the money and fame started rolling in I started losing track of who I was. That's the critical time. You have to be able to tell yourself: "If they take it all away from me now, I still have me." You gotta believe that.'

He said his own basic values and Scientology helped him survive. 'A guy can only take so much. You have to stop or you find you aren't the same guy you were before.' As he was searching for a home and using the Church of Scientology for support, the British Ministry of Health had condemned Scientology as 'harmful and foreign' and banned Scientologists from entering Britain.

In May 1996, Scientology retained a controversial following in Britain. But that month the Independent Television Commission (ITC) lifted an advertising ban imposed three years earlier. The Church – denying claims it operated like a cult –

celebrated the chance to reach thousands of potential recruits.

But the UK Cult Information Centre which monitor the activities of new religions was shocked by the ITC ruling. General secretary Ian Haworth said, 'The Scientologists will obviously use this decision to present themselves in a favourable way to society which may lead to further recruitment.' The Scientologists who argued that the ban was discriminatory had fought a successful legal battle from their UK headquarters in East Grinstead, West Sussex. The ITC decided to rescind the ban after taking advice from legal experts and a professor of sociology.

In the early days of Travolta's membership Scientology was generally accepted as a do-it-yourself mental welfare kit, a compound of religion and philosophy. When Travolta was told of the British ban in 1979, he replied, 'I can't understand the hostility. The technique is so wonderful.' Interestingly, he went on, 'In Scientology you are supposed to help each other but because I am under such pressure in my working life I am a receiver not a giver. So I have to pay.'

Four years later he would skirt around how much he had paid over the years and said, 'I don't see it as giving money; you are exchanging services.' He was asked, 'Ten thousand dollars? Twenty thousand?' He replied, 'Maybe in that ballpark, yeah.' He was asked if Scientology had used his celebrity for its own purposes and said, 'I've been something of an ostrich about how it's used me because I haven't investigated exactly what the organisation's done. One part of me says that if somebody gets some good out of it maybe it's all right. The other part of me says that I hope it uses some taste and discretion. I wish I could defend Scientology better but I don't think it even deserves to be defended in a sense.'

Later he would support it eloquently. Most recently, in 1996, he tried to explain being a Catholic and a Scientologist: 'It's nondenominational. You can be Jewish or Catholic or Protestant and still be a Scientologist. It doesn't interfere with that necessarily. But once you move into the spiritual realm then it has to be designated as a religion. That's why people get confused.

'Five years ago the onus was taken off when the government *officialised* it as a religion. It's working for people and it's getting bigger and bigger. And more popular. And it's advertised a lot. There's a lot of things that are now less mysterious, if you will.'

But back in 1979, either with or without the support of Scientology, Travolta wanted to stop the world – and escape.

Chapter Fourteen

Casa Travolta

'I really want to be left alone.'

John Travolta, 1979

The getaway he craved was in the hills north of Santa Barbara: El Adobe Tajiguas was a 17-acre spread, garnished with lemon groves and avocado trees and edged by bright, flaming jungles of bougainvillaea; a $1.5 million retreat with rich trappings. It had everything except a landing strip: 'What happened was I found a place so beautiful that it upstaged the idea of having a runway on the property.'

By then *Fever* and *Grease* had grossed more than $500 million internationally and he had had his hefty slice of Hollywood action. If some people found him as cranky as Sinatra or as reclusive as Garbo, his bankers found him financially rock solid. His boast was, 'I can do anything I want to.'

There was just that little matter of *American Gigolo*. He owed Paramount a picture for that, and yet another as part of the compromise agreement for him 'walking' from the role of the elegant lover boy. This worried him as he 'rested' at the five-bedroom house.

He had two guest houses on the property and sometimes Marilu Henner would visit. By then she was dating actor Frederic Forrest, who had made a strong impression opposite Bette Midler in 1979's *The Rose*.

Travolta said, 'Marilu and I had always been friends. We'd been able to either sleep with each other or not depending on what was going on. Most of the time when we were hanging out we were, but there have been times when we were involved with other people. We were people who would get back together between relationships.'

Several other people visited as well and Travolta found himself becoming increasingly sociable. Friends arrived and played tennis or hit the swimming pool or watched movies in the screening room. They could also play with the dogs until one day an English setter bit Travolta on the lip and the dogs were sent away. He had ten stitches in the wound and it gave him something else to worry about it. He stared at it in the mirror every morning. But at least this was one hurt he could physically salve.

He had bought the ranch furnished but added his own touches, like a gift from Robert Stigwood – a Paul Jasmin drawing of Travolta. In the first months he enjoyed the seclusion, then the friends and slowly life itself. But months still followed months. He reflected on life and death: 'I know I've lived before. And I know I've been born again. There's no doubt about it. I believe in life after death. I lost my mother and Diana but I made no attempt to contact them. You see, I believe that when a person leaves their body their spirit goes directly into the next life, into the body of a newborn baby, and that no attempt should be made to hold on to them or communicate with them.

'You would draw on their energy by trying to hold on to them and they need all the strength they've got to move into the next life cycle. I believe implicitly in reincarnation and I know I'll live forever.

'That's why I'm not frightened of dying. I'm just very curious to see what is on the other side. The way I look at it there's the "genes cycle" and the "spirit cycle". One simply enters the other for a lifetime and then departs.

'When you enter the spirit world anything is possible. I don't know how many times I've lived before but it goes back a long way. I believe I was a film actor in the 1920s, in the silent movie days. I also happen to think I could have been Valentino. I get visions, dreams, images. Day and night. It's a big, big subject and hard to explain. I found out when someone told me to close my eyes and then open them and look at something. I found myself looking at a big black cat. I was told it was my spirit that had entered my body and was viewing life from a different vantage point. It began from there.'

Travolta had, of course, visited fortune tellers, often with Marilu Henner, who is a firm believer in horoscopes and things mystical, and says he has an open mind on all such questions. With Scientology he has been almost a 100 percent supporter, apart from a period in the early 80s when he felt that the Church had strayed from the teachings of its founder, L. Ron Hubbard. In 1983 he said that he disagreed with the *management* of Scientology.

Then he told writer Margy Rochlin, 'There was a period of time when Hubbard left the lines and there was this infiltration of certain personalities that disrupted the organisation. I decided that I was going to use the technology – I have all the books – and when they cleaned up their act I'd come back. Hubbard has been back for about a year now and it's been great again.'

Despite the doubts and fears of others, Travolta has always been willing to talk about Scientology. Asked to explain it in simple terms he said, 'Basically you sit opposite a person called an auditor with what we call an E-meter – a little oval shaped machine that has a meter and a needle that registers when you hold it like a little steel can. You just go through what you haven't said to people that you should have, what you did to people, what I might have done to you that bothers you, what upsets I have with people that bother me.

'There are basically three what we call "ruds" – ruds means basics. OK things get out of whack when you flaunt your ruds – upsets with people that involve a breaking of affection with them, a breaking of communication with them, a breaking of your point of view versus my point of view – your reality versus my reality.

'That's really the basics, what Scientologists call ARC – affinity, reality, communication. An auditor might say, "Did you have an ARC break?" I might say: "I had an ARC break with my brother." The auditor will ask if it was a break with affinity or affection or what. You go one at a time. Suppose you say it was a break in communication. Now the E-meter registers but you have to confirm it, agree with it. It's harder work than dancing.

'I can do it on my own. I can hold the machine without an auditor and do it. See, it's not so different from the Catholic confessional. You go over what we call "overts" which is a counter-survival act against somebody else. So they say, "Have you committed any overts today?" It's almost like saying, "Have you committed a venal sin?" except it's more objective. That's because it's what *you* consider a sin not what somebody else does – no outside-imposed rules.

'What concerns me about what people say about Scientology is that they don't acknowledge that there's bad and error in every institution – every institution can be perverted.

'My mother was a devout Catholic; she understood that Scientology wasn't a substitute for religion. It's self-help. She could live with that. You know that quote I love so much, that "Love is a continual desire to see someone else survive", it's from L. Ron Hubbard.'

In 1991, America's *Time* magazine published a damning cover story on the Church of Scientology. Writer Richard Behar did not mince words:

'Scientology, started by science–fiction writer L. Ron Hubbard to "clear" people of unhappiness, portrays itself as a religion. In reality the church is a hugely profitable global racket that survives by intimidating members and critics in a Mafia-like manner. At times during the past decade, prosecutions against Scientology seemed to be curbing its menace. Eleven top Scientologists, including Hubbard's wife, were sent to prison in the early 1980s for infiltrating, burglarising and wiretapping more than 100 private and government agencies in attempts to block their investigations.

'In recent years hundreds of longtime Scientology adherents – many charging that they were mentally or physically abused – have quit the church and criticised it at their own risk. Some have sued the church and won; others have settled for amounts in excess of $500,000. In various cases judges have labelled the church "schizophrenic and paranoid" and "corrupt, sinister and dangerous."

'Yet the outrage and litigation have failed to squelch Scientology. The group, which boasts 700 centres in 65 countries, threatens to become more insidious and pervasive than ever.

'In Hollywood, Scientology has assembled a star–studded roster of followers by aggressively recruiting and regally pampering them at the church's Celebrity Centres, a chain of clubhouses that offer expensive counselling and career guidance. Rank-and-file members, however, are dealt a less glamorous Scientology.

'According to the Cult Awareness Network, whose 23 chapters monitor more than 200 "mind–control" cults, no group prompts more telephone pleas for help than does Scientology. Says Cynthia Kisser, the network's Chicago-based executive direct, "Scientology is quite likely the most ruthless, the most classically terroristic, the most litigious and most lucrative cult the country has ever seen. No cult extracts more money from its members." Vicki Aznaran, who was one of Scientology's six key leaders until she bolted from the church in 1987 agrees. "This is a criminal organisation, day in and day out." '

The magazine also quoted Travolta, who made clear the reasons for his involvement. 'Scientology just contains the secrets of the universe. That may be hard for people to handle sometimes, hearing that.'

To a lesser degree Travolta had heard many of the claims before but often he was thrown by some allegations. The *Time* article contained one section on him which said, 'High-level defectors claim that Travolta has long feared that if he defected details of his sexual life would be made public.'

It then quoted Scientology's former chairman of the board, William Franks, as saying, 'There were no outright threats made but it was implicit. If you leave they immediately start digging up everything.'

Of all the allegations made against the Church in the article it was the claim that Travolta was a victim of sexual blackmail that was challenged.

Earl Cooley, the attorney for the Church, said that the statements made in *Time* regarding Travolta were 'absolutely false'. He said that Travolta's lawyers had written to *Time* refuting the charges before the publication of the article on 6 May 1991. No further action was taken.

But writer Richard Behar had already dismissed the threats to expose Travolta as 'superfluous reporting'. 'Last May a male porn star collected $100,000 from a tabloid for an account of his alleged two-year liaison with the celebrity – Travolta refused to comment and in December his lawyers dismissed questions about the subject as "bizarre".

In 1996 Travolta again confronted the Scientology question. He had said that Tom Cruise, Kirstie Alley and himself were 'too bold' to be manipulated by Scientology leaders. Asked about the 'Stick around because you owe us' situation he replied, 'It's more like it works so good and you feel so much better that you want to stick around.'

He said he was then a 'Thetan' and explained, 'A Thetan is the spirit. I could be higher but I'm one of those guys who really likes to get everything out of something so I don't move on until I really get it.

'Tom Cruise and I are at the same level but he did his over a two-year period fulltime. And I did mine over a longer period of time. He has training in different areas than I do. You might go and sign up for different courses than I would sign up for. It's like a university. People go with different interests. Some people go to be better in business, other people go in with family issues, others with career stuff, art stuff, physical injuries. A lot of people go in because they've had an incident they want to handle, an accident or something.'

He said that if he and Cruise met socially, 'We would probably first go into our career and family and then would go,"What are you doing now in Scientology?" And then, "Oh, that's cool. I did that." Or, "I haven't done that yet. How is it?".

'It's that simple.'

It's not of course. Especially if you are Tom Cruise or John Travolta. As well as those critical of Scientology, the two stars have also had to deal with rumours that they are gay. As Cruise's big-screen version of the the television series *Mission Impossible* broke all existing box office records in May 1996, an American magazine headline read, 'Tom Cruise's Real Life Mission Impossible: Killing Off Gay Rumours.'

Cruise and his wife Nicole Kidman, who have two adopted children, were upset by an article in *McCall's* magazine in 1995 which said that their marriage had been 'arranged'. They demanded and received a written apology and retraction from the magazine. In an interview to promote the Brian De Palma-directed *Mission Impossible* published in the June 1996 issue of *Vanity Fair* magazine Cruise was quoted as saying of the gay rumours, "I feel very angry about it. I just try to remind Nicole it's like a mantra, "You have me, you have the kids. It doesn't matter what anyone else thinks." I know it's all part of it but it's hard.'

Travolta had confronted these rumours two decades earlier but now he had more important things to worry about. He said at the time: 'Think of the last five years of my life: the highs, the awards, the deaths, the failures, everything. It's like a whirlwind and you wonder why it's happening. It's as if I've lived the life of a 50-year-old. That's when all these things usually happen to people. None of what happened to me on the personal side has happened to Burt Reynolds or Clint Eastwood or Warren Beatty. I sometimes wonder why I became a star so quickly.

'Bob told me, "I've never seen a life so accelerated as yours. For most people the good and the bad happen at a certain rate but for you it's been boom! boom! boom!"'

With all of that, the gay rumours were simply an irritation. But in Hollywood such rumours can hurt privately – and professionally.

In that context, Travolta's attitude to the gay question has really been remarkable. Is he gay?

'They say that about me, Marlon Brando, every male, especially the first year you become a star. It wears off after a while but I've heard it said about just about everybody. The rumours don't bother me – not really – because they were so extraordinary. The gay rumour about male stars is such a classic that it didn't surprise me to hear it about me because I'd heard about the others. All I thought was, "Oh, I see the game now."

The game was still being played in 1996 and by then Travolta was disdainful of it. Why did he believe it kept being mentioned? 'I think it varies depending on the intent of the interviewer. Some people might look at is as a way of lessening my reputation – and other people may look at it as heightening the reputation.'

But all those years earlier in Santa Barbara County, it was his reputation as a Hollywood superstar that was on the line. He couldn't play Garbo forever. And he owed Paramount that movie.

Chapter Fifteen
The Disco Kid

'You're a real cowboy?'

Debra Winger to John Travolta, *Urban Cowboy*,1980

Travolta's life had begun to settle, and although there were some more personal changes, these were only minor setbacks. His father had remarried only seven months after Helen Travolta's death and his new wife, June, had nursed Travolta's mother. If there was any resentment, however, it was never shown publicly. 'Look, life can go on – it must go on. Love is creative. His marrying again was a compliment to my mother. It was like, "Hey, that worked for all these years I want it again". '

Just like Travolta wanted hassle-free adulation once more. He'd received some good advice from James Cagney, who visited him at home to talk about *Cagney*, a movie script of his early life. Somehow *Life* magazine was there to record the event and the photographs of Cagney at 81 and Travolta were wonderful. 'Cagney's my biggest fan. He thinks I'm great,' Travolta said, a line that was used as part of the caption material. 'This way, buttercup,' he said to Cagney, in an effort to coax the veteran star into a better camera angle. When Travolta complained about his hair being in his eyes Cagney told him, 'Get rid of it.'

Later, Travolta would talk of this 'royal' visit. 'He came for tea and stayed for three days. He said they were three of the nicest days of his life. I said to him, "Truly, Mr Cagney?" He said, "I wouldn't lie to you son".

Years earlier Travolta's mother had. When he was misbehaving she would fake phone calls to Cagney and say, 'Mr Cagney wants you to brush your teeth; Mr Cagney wants you to go to bed.'

The *Life* magazine people told Cagney about that: 'Ah yes, it's a sweet story, isn't it?' He knew all about it – Travolta had been there first. He had asked Cagney to do his walk, the limp he had used opposite Doris Day in 1955's *Love Me or Leave Me,* and to talk about all the others – the grapefruit in Mae Clark's face in *Public Enemy* in 1931, the walk up the wall in *Yankee Doodle Dandy.* The two men from vastly different generations of Hollywood traded stories and dance steps.

Travolta showed Cagney what he had learned for *Urban Cowboy*, the movie he had finally decided to do for Paramount. Robert Evans was the producer and James Bridges (whom Travolta had met on the set of *The China Syndrome* when visiting the movie's star, Jane Fonda) was the director.

Bridges and Travolta made an interesting partnership: the cerebral director and the stud-cast actor. Travolta explained his choice: 'There was an excitement of doing a totally different kind of character for me. The setting was good. There was great dancing and music – an appealing package.'

The package included newcomer Debra Winger, one of the most individual and talented actresses of Travolta's generation. They were cast in something of a modern Western *Saturday Night Fever*. He was Bud Davis, the petrochemical worker grinding out his daily hours but reaching for the legend of the West at a Houston honky-tonk, and she was Sissy, the girl he impulsively marries. The action focuses on 'Gilley's saloon', the world's largest country and western bar run by country singer Mickey Gilley, where the entertainment highlight is a mechanical bull. Or, rather, the 'cowboys' who attempt to ride it. A replica bull costing $3,000 was sent to Travolta's Californian ranch for him to practise on.

Taken from an *Esquire* magazine article written by Aaron Latham, the script, written by Latham and James Bridges, focuses on the frontier fantasies of workers who want to escape their drudgery, just as Tony Manero had wanted to be free of Brooklyn. But Bud Davis wants more too.

He believes Sissy has been unfaithful, kicks her out of their mobile home and links up with Madolyn Smith's huffy hussy who has a 'thing' for cowboys. Sissy moves in with the brilliant Scott Glenn as Wes Hightower, a macho former convict who also happens to control the bull rides at Gilley's.

Audiences soon know that there's not going to be a High Noon. It's more High 10 p.m. coming up on the electronic bull, which bucks as hard as a real one. This is a manhood test. Figuratively. And, if you land wrong, literally.

But before that, the new couples become rivals on the dance floor in the rowdy atmosphere of rodeo and beer guzzling. The Texas Shuffle is their weapon: the man holds onto the woman's hair and the woman hooks both thumbs into the man's belt loops while a long-necked bottle of Texan 'Lone Star' beer protrudes symbolically from the man's pocket.

If that sounds simple but primitive you should have been on location. The filming of *Urban Cowboy* is a legend to many Hollywood veterans. They have 'I survived…' T-shirts. Like all good battles it had a civilised beginning.

Travolta and James Bridges travelled to Houston by rail in a club carriage once owned by Howard Hughes. It had bedrooms, a kitchen and sitting room and fully-trained staff. Bridges was impressed with Travolta for making such Old World arrangements. He was following his success with *China Syndrome*, which had been a triumph for him and its stars Jane Fonda, Jack Lemmon and Michael Douglas. He wanted to prove that he was as gifted as he appeared. Travolta wanted to re-establish his initial huge success.

But this was an uneasy Travolta. Robert Evans was co-producing with music mogul Irving Azoff (his acts, including Jimmy Buffett, The Eagles, Dan Fogelberg, Boz Scaggs and Joe Walsh, would be on the movie soundtrack) and thought he had seen it all. Chrissakes, he'd *dealt* with it all.

Some scenes highlighted the predicament of Evans – a very adroit and urbane shit-kicker – in this make-believe world of macho and pointed cowboy boots, which was seemingly becoming real. One took place at the jammed Gilley's when a VIP crowd like Andy Warhol and Diane Von Furstenburg were close to the stage. Suddenly there was a cry: 'Give the guy some air!'

Mickey Gilley shouted again, his concern for Travolta mounting: 'Air! Give the guy some air! Are you trying to make him another Elvis?'

Travolta could have gone that way. He himself said, years later, that fame-game boys like him are usually dead by or before forty or, at a push, fifty. (Ironically Hollywood super-producer Don Simpson of *Top Gun*, and *Beverly Hills Cop*, was then the production chief at Paramount and taking flak over the *Urban Cowboy* budget. He barely made it to fifty before the pressure and – in his case – the drinks and drugs caught up in 1995.) Gilley's was a metaphor for all that. Here were people trying to take pieces off him. Travolta – not the bull – was the meat.

Travolta was hiding behind an untidy beard and attitude; he ordered that the set be closed to the press so, with nothing official to write, the speculation grew along with his beard. The location had a fortress mentality. Arrangements for promotional photographs and interviews were shelved. There was confusion over the film's budget, which finally reached $13 million.

As filming went on the stories got sillier. So did the situations: one almost shut down the film. Evans – almost banished from his own film set – finally broke all the rules and snarled to the *Los Angeles Times*: 'I've had a major altercation over Travolta's beard. I insisted his beard come off and Travolta and all his people were very upset. I'm making one Travolta picture in my career and I want him without a beard.'

Bob Le Mond tried to patch over what to onlookers was a petty argument. He suggested that Travolta was sensitive about a mark left by the dog bite in Santa Barbara. Everyone else apparently thought he was just intolerable. The beard stayed on for some filming and then came off. A childish compromise.

Later, a more mellow Evans offered, 'He was scared after *Moment by Moment*. It was his way of hiding.'

Travolta, though, was going about his business in a most business-like way. He learned to use a lasso, the steps for the 'Cotton-Eyed Joe' dance and even to ride the bull ('It really bruises up your legs and your butt but I got over it quick') and coped well with an outbreak of flu that downed him, James Bridges and Debra Winger. Many suggest it was Winger who made Travolta look good in *Urban Cowboy*. It was certainly her breakthrough film and she stamped her card in Hollywood with her sexy, raspy voice and unique sensuality.

At the time Travolta did not realise how lucky he was to be working with her. She won better notices than her co-star. Later, she allowed Richard Gere literally to sweep her off her feet in *An Officer and a Gentleman* – which Travolta had turned down – and won a Best Actress Oscar nomination. She joined the Oscar race again as Shirley MacLaine's tragic daughter in *Terms of Endearment* in which she won the admiration of Jack Nicholson and drew the now classic line from her co-star and Oscar rival Ms MacLaine: 'Dear, brilliant, turbulent Debra marches to a different drummer than the rest of us.' The irony of that remark from mystical MacLaine was not lost on Debra Winger.

Down-to-earth Winger, who has intimidated Hollywood and most of its men since *Urban Cowboy*, just lets a smile play around her face at Jack Nicholson's claim that he's the only male not frightened by her, and his insistence that they are twin rebel souls.

'I think he meant that as a compliment,' said Winger, whose favourite film review is one that called her 'a fetching little slut'. It was she who turned on a Texas bar as she mounted the mechanical bull and turned it into an erotic display as, fast and slow, in skintight red pants, a sheer top and high heels, she rode it in *Urban Cowboy*.

Hollywood regards her as eccentric because she chases her feelings rather than the bottom line, the almighty dollar. She rejected Steven Spielberg's offer to be in the original *Raiders of the Lost Ark*, turned down the Kathleen Turner temptress role in *Body Heat* ('I thought they were going to use this second-rate actor in the lead' – it was Oscar winner William Hurt) and absolutely believes in freedom to make *her* choices.

Often they are original; often they are not commercial.

'I figure I'm old enough. I get to do that now. I was lucky coming out of the pen pretty early on in my career to have big successes and that's fine and I happen to like some of the movies as well. That's just luck but I just didn't feel I had to be part of the machine anymore. I've been having a great time doing what I chose and I chose what I did because of where I was in my personal life. It has always been that.

It never has been for my career – I've always chosen a film because I wanted to explore that part of humanity.'

A tough cookie, she has never said a word against Travolta. It is not her style. She suffered the movie location the same way as the flu. Quietly. What she doesn't say says everything.

But in that humid heat in Houston – this was not Ralph Lauren cowboy country – Travolta had a circle of advisers. Should he do this? Or that? An interview? A photo session? If he did it went wrong. If he didn't he felt he should have. He thought he would look stupid dancing the 'Cotton-Eyed Joe'. He didn't. He demanded to see tape of his dance sequences. Video replays in his trailer reassured him. As did Texas choreographer Patsy Swayze – the wife of a young dancer-actor called Patrick Swayze.

Later, one critic would single out his 'raw, narcissistic sexuality – a sexuality so intimate and exposed it's almost embarrassing to look at – that evokes the first great male sex object of the movies, Valentino'.

But in the rainswept, flooded Texas location he felt about as alluring as Fred Flintstone. Everybody around would have been more comfortable in a cartoon. Travolta's camp portray him as the true-grit tenderfoot who had to deal with it all. The press hailed him as the 'Rhinestone Cowboy'.

He was more the Disco Kid.

At Gilley's, film extras – real customers and movie fans keen on free beer and some moments in the camera lights – would often get verbal after liberal gulps of Lone Star. They claimed Travolta was 'an asshole'. They went for his ego. He couldn't fly pussy never mind planes. And that was about as sophisticated as the redneck humour became. Travolta heard it all, and those on the set say that the only catcalls that really annoyed him were about his flying prowess. He had no qualms about the bucking bull.

'The first night I went down to Gilley's with Travolta we slipped in a side door to show John exactly what it looked like. Before we could stop him he was on the dance floor,' said James Bridges: 'He had a beard then and nobody noticed him. But the moment we were in the "hot" area around the bull people began to recognise him. There were catcalls, the redneck honky-tonkers baiting him while their girls screamed with excitement. A little too much macho tension there.

'I was in there one night when there were fifteen fights. I was there one night when someone's eyes were gouged. And I was there when Steve Strange, who runs the bull, threw a guy on and said to me: "Watch!". And he took the controls and threw him up in the air. The guy's back fell against the plastic base of the bull and he split his head open. There was blood everywhere – everybody thought he was dead. They got him up after about fifteen minutes. Steve walked over laughing, poured beer on the base of the bull to wash the blood off and then turned around and shouted, "Next." '

Travolta knew all this. 'The people who hung out there were ready to fight – definitely. But I liked it. I got a real charge out of that *danger*.'

James Bridges was not so keen, especially on the mechanically driven bull: 'It isn't easy to ride that thing and I promise you I wouldn't go near it. It scared me to death. In the end John rode it better than anyone else in Gilley's – and at top speed. They say that if the man operating the bull's controls wants you off there's no way you can stay on. John did. When we shot the big sequence in the film where he rides the bull he did it so well that all the other bull riders applauded.'

It was a big moment. But Bridges believes the movie was to be part of the Travolta myth – had to be part of it: 'You know, you have to play the cowboy – it has certified all the major stars. McQueen, Newman, Brando – they all had to play that American hero to solidify their careers forever.'

Away from the set, though, Travolta seemed to be on the look out for trouble. One – anonymous – producer was quoted as saying he was 'the most paranoid star in Hollywood today' and 'worse than Streisand and Sinatra combined'. Certainly there had been star demands like a private chef, home and flights during the location shooting. His trailer became his cocoon.

Nearer to home things got worse. Travolta inadvertently got caught in the crossfire of Los Angeles gang warfare.

The *Urban Cowboy* moviemakers had set up their cameras in the Pico Rivera section of Los Angeles – right on top of gang territory. That was enough to get the 'gang-bangers' to go for their weapons. By their code *no one* wanders on to their turf and for them to allow it would be to lose face with other gangs. Half a dozen men were picked to 'take-out' the location. Armed with sawn-off rifles – more effective at a distance than 'shooter shotguns' – they sprayed the location camp with bullets. It was a hit-and-run shooting spree. They were gone before the police emergency calls were completed.

The effect on Travolta lasted much longer. Paramount Pictures security guard Jerry Ray recalled the attack: 'There were six men – three of them were fully armed. Any one of their shots could have killed somebody. All of us were afraid, including Travolta. It's not nice having gunfire going off thirty feet from you. Every shot sounds like an explosion. Travolta was real upset there were guns near him – he's real afraid of them. The gang had been making threats earlier at the parking area where we had all our equipment. I was threatened and they said they would return and shoot their way in to the closed-off area. They just didn't like the idea of

Travolta and the crew tying up their zones. I don't recall it as being anything personal against Travolta.'

But Robert Evans' recollection was, 'They just started shooting and Travolta was so convinced the gang was out for his blood that he ordered an end to the location sequence. We had to lose two days' shooting of our movie before we could get into the Paramount Studio lot where there was sufficient protection from the guards. John said he couldn't do the scene under the conditions of stress and fear after the shooting attack.'

Travolta seemed a different person. He was close to Scientology minister the Rev Heber Jentsch, whose remarks did not amuse Hollywood: 'There are tremendous responsibilities being laid on the shoulders of this young man. Of course you start to wonder how long it will last and so Scientology is setting up goals beyond where he currently is. I know he will be prepared to handle it all.' But was he?

Shortly after the shooting incident his sister Annie said, 'There have been times when he seems at a complete loss. He was never like this before. Usually he's happy-go-lucky. Not now.'

Travolta sought intense Scientology counselling. He was being protected, said the newspapers, like Howard Hughes had been by the Mormon Mafia in Utah. It seemed a little over-the-top but then Travolta himself said: 'At premières and parties I suddenly see what all this fame means and it frightens me, the physical force of it all. I am scared that something will happen to me.'

He hired bodyguards for public outings. He got involved in many Scientology sessions. Out came the E-meter. 'You're going to get rid of the bullshit and that's it. It is a way of pinpointing where you're blocked – you leave a session resolved.' The security on *Urban Cowboy* – the moonlighting Texas cops, the beefed-up Paramount patrols – was mirrored at his hacienda in Santa Barbara.

But guards, like guns, can go off prematurely. After a Golden Globe Awards ceremony at the Beverly Hilton, Travolta was being driven away from the hotel's VIP parking area next to the hotel's in-house Trader Vic's restaurant. Photographer Todd Wallace, a callow 17-year-old, was trying to take a picture when a bodyguard, a bearded brick-wall, wiped him out of the way. Ace paparazzo Ron Gallela took a photograph of the incident. The picture was published worldwide, whereupon Wallace filed a million-dollar lawsuit (settled out of court), and Travolta went on the run.

Joey Travolta worried about his baby brother, 'John's too introverted and non-assertive.' Marilu Henner was with him again but there seemed only turmoil. Travolta complained, 'There are very few people to whom I can say whatever is in my heart.'

American television star Freddie Prinze – just a couple of years older than Travolta – had blown his brains out because, his friends said later, he felt 'lost with fame'. Travolta and others on the *Kotter* set formed a Samaritan agreement: they would telephone each other if depression ever made them suicidal.

In the malignant world of Hollywood that could easily have happened. The Hollywood Women's Press Club – the inheritors of the 'malice in wonderland' gossip queens, Louella Parsons and Hedda Hopper – gave him their 'Sour Apple Award' as the actor 'most likely to believe his own publicity'. Others were also serving poison about him from decanters. He just wasn't drinking it. Or anything else:

'They were waiting for me to go on some drinking binge or end up on a drugs charge. God knows, it had been hard enough on me without all that. Very hard. It was really scary, being grabbed, crushed and pushed around.

'One minute everything... and the next... I suppose if there is an explosion in the positive area there had to be an explosion of comparable magnitude in the negative area.

'If I had gone the drink-and-drug route I would have folded under. I don't want to sound good-goody but I lead a clean life. I knew from the start that wasn't the way to go. I took the time off because I was scared. I admit that. I just had to have a break. I had frightening experiences. Look, when I was in London at the *Grease* opening I thought the roof of the car was going to cave in with the fans.

'I genuinely thought my life was going to end. It was panic point for me. And yet it was exciting. Part of me was loving it and another side was wondering whether I was going to come out of it alive....'

Chapter Sixteen
Travolta Talks

'The adulation, the money,
the power can make you believe you're
somebody you're not. It's like eating a
building brick by brick. Sometimes I'm
so scared I can't spell my name.'

Henry 'The Fonz' Winkler, 1977

John Travolta was back in the Hollywood saddle following *Urban Cowboy*. Everyone connected with the movie got a strong reception. But there was still flak to deal with.

James Bridges played down all talk of 'Travolta megalomania' and Travolta himself insisted that his publicity-shyness on the movie was to allow him to concentrate on his role as city cowboy, Bud. However, while he was cementing his place in Hollywood history by getting his star, the 162nd, and putting his hand and cowboy boot prints on Hollywood's Walk of Fame, his image was being taken care of by Paramount. Publicity pictures from *Urban Cowboy* were being retouched to lose, at his insistence, his 'thunder-thighs'. His ego was reported to be as big as Texas.

Travolta, who can be hurt by a sideways glance, took all the criticism personally. He has never been able to separate it as 'just business'. Others can see it as the loose change of stardom but for him being liked was – and is – always the bottom dollar. He wants to be loved.

He met up with Muhammad Ali in Santa Barbara (there was talk of them making a movie together) and wrote a fan letter to Woody Allen, explaining, 'I'm leaning toward a comedy for my next film.'

His love life sounded farcical at times. He seemed to be in everybody's bed. One moment he was with Marilu Henner, the next he was off with Brooke Shields or Catherine Deneuve or Debra Winger or Nancy Allen or Lesley-Ann Warren or Jane Fonda. He says most of the women he dated were famous but added, 'I just never went places where we were photographed.'

On Brooke Shields, he said, 'We had something of a romance but it depends on the degree you want to get involved.'

And on Catherine Deneuve: 'Well, I saw her in France but then I also saw Gerard Depardieu and his family.'

Fonda was another matter. A fantasy: 'I had a recurring dream about her which

I won't describe other than I'm making love to her. She knows about it – she told someone she was flattered! Jane's a woman I feel has a reserved sexuality she tries to temper. I think she's probably a wild woman in bed.'

Travolta had made friends with Houston socialite Maxine Messenger during the *Urban Cowboy* filming. She had flown to Los Angeles to see her friend Barbara Stanwyck, who later talked about their evening together:

'Maxine Messenger was in town with her husband Emil and begged me to have dinner with them and John Travolta who wanted to meet me. Being a fan of Travolta's I finally capitulated and we had a lovely evening. I was impressed with John's simplicity and shyness. He was the perfect gentleman. We exchanged fond farewells before leaving the restaurant and then it became sheer pandemonium.

'As we were leaving the cafe at least twenty-five cameramen were outside trying to photograph us together. Can you just imagine those scandalous tabloids linking us together! Especially with that old gossip that Travolta liked older women?'

And Travolta wasn't alone. Marilu Henner had fallen for an older man. On 28 September 1980, she was a 28-year-old bride. Frederic Forrest at 42 was the groom. Travolta had missed out. Friends said he had taken her for granted, thinking she would 'always be there.' Her brother Tom said, 'After eight years of getting the runaround from John, in walks Fred and not only says, "I love you" but also, "I want to marry you". She was literally swept off her feet.'

Meanwhile, Travolta was alone. 'Once or twice a month I'd have four or five beers and get high. I smoke cigars now. My father smokes cigars and when I was growing up I loved the smell. I tried one then and it made me sick. But now I like them. When I was learning to fly my instructor gave me one after each lesson.'

He tried to front his lifestyle. 'My favourite time is when I get to smoke cigars and watch movies for days. It took me two days just to watch Bertolucci's *1900*. I had a ball. Nobody bothered me. I'd eat by myself, take a couple of cigars and go up to the screening theatre. I sat there and said: "Oh, this is the life!" '

Of course, it wasn't the life he wanted. Kate Edwards was around and so was Jerry Wurms, acting as an unofficial bodyguard. But, of course, Marilu Henner wasn't. Later, he talked about her first marriage: 'It was a total surprise. We hadn't really been seeing each other regularly at the time but I was still shocked and sad. I felt a real loss. For the two years she was married we didn't see each other.

'I missed her a lot. But I always thought I'd have her as a friend and would just have to deal with not being able to sleep with her. Bottom line, I'll always have Marilu as a friend because we've made a pact never to desert each other regardless of what happens on the romantic front. Our relationship has outlasted many marriages. If I have a sexual attraction for someone I can keep it for years. Whatever it was about them that got me turned on usually continues to keep me turned on. I'm very committed to my sexual desires.'

Women have been a constant theme in his life. He thinks about them a lot and admits, 'I have a strong sex drive but it needs to be unleashed by someone who likes it. Otherwise I tend to inhibit it. I like being with women who have the same sexual appetite. I get frustrated if they don't because it's very difficult for me to be with someone I have to coach. You know, "OK, honey, I'm the sex master here, and I'll go through the paces and together we will solve your psychological blocks."

'I can't do that. So I'm usually attracted to women who have big sexual appetites and fewer sexual hang-ups.'

In the aftermath of *Urban Cowboy* he also admitted, 'I'm very alone but there's a difference between loneliness and alone. I don't feel lonely. I just feel alone. This may sound ridiculous at my age but I've lived a very fulfilled life. I've been able to achieve many of my goals, but there will always be new goals. Marriage and children are high on the list. The day I find out my wife is pregnant, I'll be a maniac. Every time I get visions of being a father I get shivers.

'Of course I want the right woman but I'm not in the mood to go look for her. I'm being sort of reclusive. To be really honest, I'd have to say I'm afraid to commit to one person, so I have maybe three or four people on the line. But it's very uncomfortable to me now.

'With a career, you're depending on your own ability – not someone else's – to get you through. Love takes two; your career takes one. And with love, there's always another fish in the sea.

'I have such a high opinion of women that my expectancy level is also high. I expect them to be intelligent and very career-orientated. If they want a family, fine, but that doesn't mean giving up goals. Bottom line, a woman's gotta be stimulating, which would then provoke a continuous sexual appeal. I have less tolerance with women than I do with men. I can tolerate a man's not being bright or ambitious but not a woman's.

'It began with my mother and sisters. I grew up around women who were colourful, exciting, inspiring. I have an innate understanding of what women do. I allow them much more grace than most men would. I like everyone I'm involved with, and I never want to lose those friendships. Romance has a tendency to confuse friendships, and I don't want that. With Diana her being eighteen years older was certainly a built-in barrier. I was incredibly mad for this woman and the age thing, because it was awkward in society's eyes, only made the relationship more titillating to me.

'I felt that and openly admitted it – after the fact. But it's a complicated statement. Who knew what that would've led to especially with her being older and ill? In my heart I felt I wanted to marry her but again there were those barriers.

'I love Marilu. It depends on your definition of love. I don't mean to sound whimsical or neurotic but I've discovered that because my life is malleable and gypsylike I have the ability to feel like I'm in love with a few people at the same time. It's not as if I'm a farmer. If I were, I'd have no problem being with one person, committing to that lifestyle. But I'm in a business where I find it very hard, at this point, to be monogamous.

'So, yes, I could say I'm in love with Marilu, even though that doesn't mean I'm not in love with other people on some level, too. The one thing Marilu and I have in common is that we know each other so well that she could even hear this conversation and it would be okay.

'I've wanted to come clean about my situation for a long time, especially with Marilu. And I did, and she did the same with me, so who knows what happens next? The only voice bothering me is the one that says, "You're going to lose everybody." Every day it's different. I do think I'd like to get married, but mainly to have children. If I weren't having children then I don't know how compelled I'd feel to get a piece of paper.

'By nature I don't think man is monogamous even though by agreement he tries to be. By nature I am not monogamous but by agreement – and ideal – I am.

'I've always been crazy about women, ever since I was a little kid. In my family women were special – my mother, Helen, and my sisters, Ellen, Margaret and Annie, gave me lots of affection. Even as I got older and most boys started to go through a stage where they thought girls were yukky, I thought they were terrific.

'That doesn't mean I always understood them, though. When I was about 12 I had a crush on this girl who liked another boy. One day, all of a sudden, she decided to be my girlfriend and I was thrilled, but within a few weeks she'd gone back to him. I think she'd only had a passing fancy for me because I was a flashy dancer and had a new navy suit.

'The funny thing is that love and romance have seemed in some ways to get more complicated and confusing as I've gotten older. When you're a teenager a love relationship is so special and idealistic, but when you get into your 20s you start discovering that there are lots of people in the world and you have lots of options; career options, romantic options. You get involved in a certain life style, and it can be difficult to get into the swing of a committed, one-to-one relationship. I actually found steady relationships easier when I was younger. I'm still a searcher, someone who seeks love with one person – but it's harder now.

'Some of the confusion has to do with the times. I think the women's movement has been very important, but I haven't liked the defensiveness on the part of some women that's come along with it. It's not that I think such feelings are inappropriate, but I've observed that sometimes there is a defiance that seems to be implied as opposed to real. I wish those women could assert themselves without giving up all the great qualities that are so individual to a woman.

'I also think that we shouldn't put so many rules on what each person in a relationship should do for the other and instead just go by the individual cases. If the man cooks better than woman, maybe he should do the cooking, and if she doesn't mind doing the laundry and he hates it, maybe she should do that. But at the same time, if they want a more traditional relationship that's okay, too. I just don't think we should say it should be *this* way or *that* way. It has to reflect what each individual has to offer and how it can all be balanced.

'I think that things would be a lot less confusing if two people in a relationship were open with each other about what they wanted. I think many women want their men to be not just their lovers but their friends as well, and to be devoted to them in a way that is more than just bringing home a pay-cheque. They want in men some of the qualities they find in their girlfriends – the ability to be affectionate, supportive and a good listener.

'I suppose that's really what a man wants from a woman but it's easier expected from a woman and easier gotten from her too. It's hard for men to be that way even with other men. We sometimes suppress our emotions; we often think it's appropriate to be affectionate in bed with a woman but not anyplace else.

'Women have an ability to speak out and be heard. They're more verbal. And sometimes it becomes a case of the squeaky wheel getting the grease. Because even though women can be very tolerant and patient, it's sometimes hard for a man to express his real feelings. With so many men I sense that below the surface there's a much more loving, caring person than there appears to be. I think women have to really help men express themselves, uncover these emotions, let them be different.

'I know, for instance, that in some relationships I've had with women there have been parts of me I wish I could have revealed but couldn't. One is a certain childlike quality, a need to be really toasty and totally affectionate in a way that might not seem at all macho. I suspect many men wish they could express certain needs to a woman, like "I'm lonely" or "Give me a hug" or "Please hold me," but they're afraid women only want to see the macho part. Because of this a man sometimes becomes father and only father, and I think that's bad, just as it's bad for a woman to be mother and only mother. Sometimes she needs to be father, just as sometimes the man needs to be mother.

'After all, how can you really know what the other sex wants unless you can experience being them? One think I liked about the movies *Tootsie* and *Victor/Victoria* is that they showed what kind of discovery there is in living like someone of the opposite·sex. It's like back massages. You can't know a good one unless you've had a back massage and know what's pleasing. Even with making love, you have to know what a woman likes and what feels good for her. So it's important to discover, to find out about what each of you needs. It's the only way that there can be pleasure and honesty and understanding.

'I know that some women have perceived me as the macho guy in control, but that's not really the case. I'm as vulnerable in a relationship as the woman is. I want to meet someone halfway; I'm not there to control things but to experience what there is to experience.

'Of course when it comes to expressing needs in a relationship it's going to make a world of difference if both of you can talk easily about such things. The problem comes when one person in a relationship is able to communicate well but the other isn't – or neither one of you can. If that's the case, then you have to find ways to make it safe for each other to communicate. You can't be critical of their truth, or judgmental if you really want them to be honest with their feelings. You have to give them the space to express themselves. In certain cases you may have to ask that person what there is about you that inhibits communicating with you. Is there a fear you'll think less of him or her? You have to make it as safe as possible.

'What turns up when you can communicate with each other can surprise you. If you discover that you have standards and prerequisites that are different from those of the person you're involved with, it may predict problems. But if you can free yourself and experience what that other person is, you may find that the joys of that person far outweigh the negatives. Sometimes you need to remove yourself from what you *think* are your priorities and look at what really is.

'When you communicate in a relationship, you also discover things about yourself. One of the biggest things I learned from a woman I loved was that when a problem occurs in life you simply have to deal with it. At one point there was some conflict that had come up with her, and I asked, "What if that happened to me?" and she said, "You'd simply have to handle it." My tendency had always been to avoid problems. The solution suddenly seemed so simple.

'When it comes to women, I certainly don't have all the answers for myself, but I'm trying. I'm working on it. I'm asking a lot of questions of women, like, "How do you feel when you do this? What do you do when that happens to you?" And I'd also actively try to make it understood what a *man* goes through, because I don't think a woman always knows.'

What Travolta also admitted in his open-hearted talk then was his passion for and love of work as well as of women: 'My driving force is maintenance – maintenance of a career. The truth is I don't need another blockbuster for my career. *Urban Cowboy* did $100 million. Now, what's wrong with that? If it had been my first movie, I'd have been a big movie star. It keeps on being compared to the first two movies, which are so mega that if I had only done one of them I'd still be okay.

'I was offered *An Officer and A Gentleman*, which I turned down, basically because I felt the girl had the best part. Anyway, after the movie came out, I said to Warren Beatty, "Do you think I should have done *An Officer and A Gentleman*?" And he said, "Why?" And I said, "Because it was a commercial success." He said, "You have two of the biggest movies in movie history. Why do you need another one? Just do good movies, John."

'And Warren, who I happen to think represents the ultimate show-business viewpoint, was right. In the list of the ten top–grossing movies of all time, I was the only actor the public came to see as an actor. The rest of the top grossers were all special-effects films – *E.T., The Empire Strikes Back, Jaws, Raiders of the Lost Ark*. I may be the only actor the public went to see instead of a shark.

'I've been called a very old young man and that is something that's been a problem for me ever since I was a kid. See, I was the youngest in my family. My mother and father were both forty-two when I was born, so by the time I started really picking up their vibes, they were already fifty. I started looking at life through their eyes, but life through fifty-year-old eyes may not be as chipper as a kid deserves to see it. What I observed was fifty-year-old parents and their anxieties, their blues, their sensing the third chapter of their lives. That's never left me, and as a result, I have always had an older person's point of view on life. In other words, I sense the end. I get blue more easily because I'm not always appreciating the youth I have.

'My mother had relentless, undying interest in my well-being and career. There's nothing like it. No one is more interested in your career and your well-being than your mother. *No one*. And I miss her being able to enjoy all of this. We came from a neighbourhood where you had dreams of having what I have. And she always did. She got to be here at the ranch for a couple of weeks and she went to the Oscars and Europe but being able to really have lived this lifestyle would've been something else. I would've gotten off watching her enjoy it.

'I disagreed with the doctor about how to treat my mother. My turmoil was more than just my mother's being at the end of her life. It was really, "Are we doing the right thing?" Her blood was not coagulating correctly, but they got it to coagulate enough to cut into her anyway. But she didn't have the healing abilities, the stamina to bear up. She should never have been opened up, and I feel I let them do it because the doctors made me feel it was okay.

'I feel responsible for that. The doctor persuaded me to have the operation, and then, when it was over, he said, "Hey, man, we're only a practice." I said, "Well, you didn't say that three weeks ago. Three weeks ago it was a demand. She must have this operation. Now, suddenly, you say you're just a practice?" We had a big fight.

'It was a rude awakening that we are always right next to death. It's a cliché, but it gave me an ability to appreciate life more and to do things I want to, within reason. Like the time I bought my plane. Financially, it was a little steep for me, but I said, "Man, flying is one of the passions of your life, so do it." And I savour people more. I appreciate how much I'm going to miss them if they or I go. I'm less afraid of dying because I accept it more as a part of life.

'When I was a teenager, I remember thinking that I did not want to leave this world without its being marked by my presence in some fashion. That was a compulsion for me. So my achievements have enabled me to be a little less afraid of death on the one hand; on the other, they also make me not want to leave because I have so much to live for.

'I always wanted to do well. Doing well to me meant having a series of Broadway shows and always being able to work. I think I had a lot of presence onstage and I was good but I don't think I had the technique to carry a serious stage career. I never had the projection to get to the back of the theatre. You had to be three rows away from me to get my performance.

'Part of what gets me through every day is reviewing it all: "John, come on. Look at what you've accomplished. Look at where you came from and where you are now. Look at the people you know, your lifestyle, the projects you've put out and the impact on society you've made." I don't want to waste it. I want to appreciate all of it. I need to continually recognise – not egotistically – but just recognise what I've already done; otherwise, I have a tendency to be hard on myself and forget what I've done, make it into something not so special so I can live with it every day.

'Being a child of the 60s and a 70s teenager made me understand my own generation, even though I was probably more career-orientated than most. But it was really through my performances that I became an archetype. Everyone could identify with me because they had a friend either like me or like one of the characters I played. I had one quality of someone that everyone knew in the 70s. I was king of the 70s.'

But now it was the 80s.

Chapter Seventeen
Staying Alive

'He was no longer a boy.'

Brian De Palma on his leading man, 1981

Good movies, sex and eating – in any order – were Travolta's diet of preference for the 80s. But out of that trio the one he couldn't buy were film roles that mattered to him, Hollywood and audiences.

No other young actor, with the exception of James Dean, had made a stronger impact in so few appearances and he was also fabulously wealthy. But for him there was clearly a lot more than love that money couldn't buy.

'You come to a point where you say, "Is this really fair?" To have all this money. In all honesty it is the American Dream but you wonder, "Is it fair for me to have it?" Not that I want to be poor but there's a little voice that begins to say: "Is this really right?" You want to help people with their dreams. Look, after *Saturday Night Fever* kids wore white suits and black shirts and thought they were John Travolta for the day. Even I wasn't John Travolta. I was an illusion created by film. It was a dream. People need their dreams.'

He also needed to commute into reality. He pondered on relationships, love and sex: 'Sometimes I think sex is separate from love. Sex is definitely an expression of love and desire and affection but sometimes I think pure love is something that's very separate from it. Sometimes I think sex is just a function, an action that is pleasurable, feels good – and especially if you care about a person. You love people and you have sex with some people that you love. You don't have sex with everybody that you love,' said Travolta, the most tactile of men.

Strangely – amazingly to those outside Hollywood – the Travolta-and-the-Beard confrontation on *Urban Cowboy* still bothered Travolta. He insisted that he had helped the movie by presenting a 'new character' in the first ten minutes. 'Everybody except Jim Bridges fought me on wearing it because of the image so I figure I got my way. Paramount were very conscious of the John Travolta image. With *Blow Out* I was totally allowed to let go of it.'

Clearly trivial to many people, this concern about 'look' reflected Travolta's seriousness about himself. His friends and co-workers all portray him as a 'fun guy' – and he has never lost his sense of humour about his fan-struck fame – but alone with his stardom he talked to the mirror. He explained it like this: 'I just don't want to lose power, don't want to blow it all, and that's why every decision gets harder.'

Blow Out was a *Carrie* reunion – Brian De Palma as director, Nancy Allen as co-star – and a departure from the swaggering macho hero of *Fever*, *Grease* and *Urban Cowboy*. It was a thinking role, distinct from the previous elemental types. Behind the casting scenes Frank Sinatra had apparently pulled strings – at the request of James Cagney – to help Travolta win the role.

'It was a step forward. I got to do things I'd never done before on film like have intelligent conversations. For a time we were all laughing because I couldn't get the speeches out of my mouth. I said to Brian: "You'll have to be patient." I was used to saying nothing much more than, "I love you." Or "I hate you". I got through it.'

The movie is one of De Palma's better dark games, a political thriller with Travolta as electronics whiz kid Jack Terri, a master of aural voyeurism. Terri had used his skills in investigating police corruption but after the death of a good cop finds himself working in cheap horror-movie sound effects. But the horror really begins one evening when he witnesses a car crash into a river. He rescues the woman passenger, played by Nancy Allen, but the driver is not just dead: he's a dead Presidential candidate. The story gets as murky as the water from then on.

It was a critical success but a commercial bomb. Years later Travolta could see it as one of his career highlights. The reviews he received were some of the best of his career. It was said that the only thing wrong with *Blow Out* was the timing. It was a 70s movie released in the 80s.

What it did do was establish his relationship with the De Palmas.

The movie reflected De Palma's fascination with Chappaquiddick, Watergate and John Kennedy's assassination and drew a worshipful critique from Pauline Kael, who praised his 'vision' and compared Travolta to 'the very young Brando'.

'I didn't write the role for John, because I thought he was too young but when we met again I saw he was no longer a boy but a grown man and quite right for it,' said De Palma, who had similarly dismissed his wife Nancy as having done too many films with him. She disagreed: 'When John said I should play the part, logic went out of the window, and I reacted emotionally. I love John, and I wanted to work with him.'

Shooting went smoothly until they had to film scenes underwater trapped in a car. 'Even though it was a five-foot deep tank at Burbank Studios I became hysterical, I'm claustrophobic,' said Allen. 'I was afraid to ask questions because I didn't want the special effects crew to think I was stupid.

'Thank God for John. He asked questions for me and taught me buddy breathing.' Travolta was so good underwater (he did his own aquatic stunts) that the crew presented him with a floating director's chair inscribed *Esther Travolta*. The movie was a happy ship and Travolta recalled:

'There was always an affinity there but then we were closer than ever.' He spent a weekend at the beach house the De Palmas rented on Long Island. 'They're loyal people to their friends. They support you totally. I feel so relaxed with them – like I could say or do anything. There's no strain at all. '

Travolta's fame created some problems for his hosts. Nancy Allen recalled, 'Just going out with John could be frustrating and imposing at times. Twenty people queue up for his autograph while you're trying to have a conversation. There is something very touchable, an openness about him. He's very sweet to his fans. He's always polite.'

He also wanted to be funny in the movies. He was actively looking for comedy material but he revealed, 'Brian wanted to do *Scarface* with me and Al Pacino but things got complicated.' The complication was the poor box office of *Blow Out*. He complained: 'I don't think anyone should be penalised for trying to change his image but whatever you do it's: "How dare you?" or, "What a fool you made of yourself." ' For many in Hollywood Travolta had more than proved he could act and didn't need to dance in a movie. But who wanted to see him act?

The fan mail at El Adobe Tajiguas, which was all catalogued by his father and stepmother June, added up to worldwide interest. So many girls broke into the ranch – even into his wardrobes hunting for intimate keepsakes – that he had to install permanent security guards.

He also wanted career security, to build on his 'serious' reviews from *Blow Out* but greenback-motivated Hollywood wanted him singing and dancing. He started flying around – anywhere, everywhere – to think clearly. He had 'adopted' yet another family in Gerard Depardieu and his wife Elizabeth. Depardieu, then best known to English-speaking audiences for 1980's *The Last Metro*, talked of them doing a movie together. They would play unlikely brothers. Travolta learned French: 'I didn't want to be rude. Why should they have to talk *my* language?' The film vanished but their friendship didn't: 'I'd always admired Gerard and when I was in Paris in the late 1970s I just walked into a restaurant in Paris where he was lunching and introduced myself. He was tickled pink and we've been friends ever since. I'd take my jet and fly over to Paris just to spend a week with him and his family. We were like brothers.'

Travolta's interests in all things French continued despite the failure of the project. His fascination for jazz violinist Stephane Grappelli inspired him to take up the violin. He took a course in new 'by-ear' music and within six weeks had a five-song repertoire including 'Ain't Misbehavin'' and, one of his mother's favourites, 'The Sunny Side of the Street'.

He was considering working with another old friend – Olivia Newton-John. He had admitted they were lovers during a British publicity tour for *Urban Cowboy* in 1980 but this new venture was to be purely professional. She said: 'We want to make a musical comedy. John has gone through more than 300 scripts but has seen nothing that interests him.'

But all Paramount Studios were interested in was getting another Travolta movie in the can. He was wary, explaining, 'I'd grasped that when you have box office potential there's very little that's not given to you. "The character's aged 70? Oh well, we'll make him your age." If you're good at the box office they'll let you make the telephone directory. '

Then, however, Travolta was ambivalent box office, although *The Godfather, Part III* was still a serious contender. Ironically, before anyone in Hollywood had heard of him – he was touring in *Grease* at the time – he had auditioned for *Godfather, Part II*. His main competition for the role of Michael Corleone's son had been Robby Benson: 'Robby had more film experience than me and got the part. They filmed scenes of him with his father but it was never put in the movie.'

Now, he was having talks and long Italian lunches with Francis Ford Coppola. And reading a 'cute' script for *Grease II*. He was talking to Jane Fonda about doing a remake (in the Jimmy Stewart role) of Frank Capra's 1939 classic *Mr Smith Goes To Washington* and to Paramount about a movie biography of 'Doors' rocker Jim Morrison. He desperately wanted to play Morrison but Paramount weren't interested. During all the talk of 'maybe' projects he turned down a hard $5 million offer to star in Richard Attenborough's screen version of *A Chorus Line*. He had also been constantly rejecting a sequel to *Saturday Night Fever*.

When he and the audience had left, Tony Manero the disco king was feeling increasingly stifled by his Brooklyn life. Soon after the film was released a script was written which Travolta ruled 'anti-dance, very cynical'. Paramount and Robert Stigwood vainly tried for two years to persuade him to film that script.

It was Catch-22. Because of his deal with Paramount he was unable to work for any other film company and he was unwilling to be involved in the projects Paramount were suggesting. He decided to go back on the stage.'I just couldn't wait any longer – that's not what this country is about. They can't tell you when you can go back to work.'

Blow Out had led to eighteen months in the career wilderness. 'The first year of not working was productive but the next six months were aggravating. Finally I decided to do a play and it all fell together. As soon as I said, "to Hell with the studio" they said, "Wait a minute, let's talk about it, John." '

But he was flying a career solo. He would do the play *Mass Appeal*, not on Broadway ('it would have attracted too much attention') but 7,908 feet above sea level in Colorado's Rocky Mountains. With veteran character actor Charles Durning he took to the boards for the first time in six years, in the two-man comedy drama explaining, 'Here you're allowed to be an artist. If we make mistakes up here it's not going to kill our careers.'

It brought him back to life. More meetings on a *Fever* sequel were arranged. There was a new script, incorporating Travolta's ideas, by Norman Wexler who had been responsible for the original. Travolta wanted Tony Manero to have a positive future. It reflected his own thinking. A deal was done.

The height – or the artistic atmosphere – gave him confidence for he said in Aspen, 'I've got more flexibility. It's been worth the wait. It was painful but it paid off to do the play. Paramount would be losing an asset if they lost me to plays. I *am* an asset to them.'

As Tony Manero was to him. He was still working in Aspen when he was told that his great supporter Michael Eisner at Paramount was going to ask Sylvester Stallone to direct the sequel to be titled *Staying Alive*.

'I had just seen *Rocky III* and had said to my agent, "This is a wild idea but if I could get that energy and excitement that's where I think this movie is going. Within a month I was meeting with Stallone. I told him what I thought was missing from the script. Norman had written a more realistic ending where Tony ends up in the chorus with the hope of someday getting something else. That might have been an interesting way for the first movie to end but not this one. For this one I wanted something more exciting. I felt you needed to put it into overdrive and send it into space. Stallone rewrote it with exactly the kind of flavour I wanted.'

Stallone felt an empathy with Travolta: 'We're in the same mould. I came out with *Rocky* in 1976 and John came out with *Fever* the next year. We both had our first biggies at the same time.'

The plan was for more biggies from this momentous collaboration, touted by some as the biggest since Scarlett met Rhett. Others found it more Laurel and Hardy. What *had* Stallone got him into?

What audiences found was polyester peacock Tony Manero half a dozen years later in the chorus line, teaching jazz class, tending bar and involved with two women, sort-of girlfriend Jackie played by Cynthia Rhodes and uppity Laura played by British actress and American soap opera graduate Finola Hughes.

Travolta and Stallone argued over the language. 'At first I didn't want to let go of the language but Stallone really talked me out of it and when I see the movie I know he was right. The first one needed the raw language because without it you wouldn't have been dealing with real kids. But when you're not a teenager anymore you stop punctuating your sentences with profanity. There are more important things to attend to than impressing your friends with the way you talk.

'Every time my instincts went toward the teenage reaction Stallone would say, "No, no, you're a man now. It's been six years. Remember that." I hadn't lived those six years for the character so my tendency was to pick up just where I left off. Whenever I went into that mode Sly toned it down. I know people like Tony in the first movie but I think they were reacting to a sort of insistent sexual presence that almost forced you to pay attention. With the sequel he was pulling people in more subtly.'

For *Staying Alive* he was leaner, more muscular: The Disco Kid by way of Charles Atlas. He lost twenty pounds in weight and built up his arms, chest and legs to get a professional dancer's body. He didn't see it at the time but he was still being marketed as a sex symbol – just in a different shape. And just as technology can overtake its subject so the Stallone-designed lean machine overwhelmed the storyline and the acting. Travolta appeared in publicity poses like an oiled Mr Universe contestant. He had worked hard for the image.

'People like Sly can look at a body like clay and mould it. I never thought of designing a body. I just thought, "Diet, run, lose it and you'll look good." I didn't think of shaping the shoulder, the triceps, the waist.'

Dan Isaacson, his trainer, did. 'John thought he would have to just do some running, sit-ups and push-ups to get ready for the role,' Isaacson recalled. 'I don't think he had an idea of what he was in for.'

What he was in for was Isaacson's arduous – sometimes torturous – programme, specially designed to turn the bulky, round-shouldered, proletarian Travolta into a hunk.

Isaacson – Height: 5-feet 7; Weight: 155; Chest: 42 inches; Waist: 30 1/2 inches – was the athletic consultant to a club in Snowmass when he and Travolta first met. While appearing in *Mass Appeal* Travolta visited the club to do a little shaping up.

'We did a lot of basic stuff for a couple of weeks he was there. When we concluded he asked me to be his trainer for *Staying Alive*,' said Isaacson who met with Stallone and the two of them designed Travolta's training programme, for which the studio would foot the bill. 'John has always been known for his great legs and his lower torso and and he has a long muscle structure, which gives him a lot of grace. But we needed to do a lot of work on his upper body in order for him to project a great presence onstage.'

Travolta sequestered himself in Santa Barbara for the first part of the training.

Isaacson moved into the guest house, bringing with him a truckload of equipment – a Universal Gym, dumbbells and barbells – to be set up in the main house.

'John's day began about 7.30 a.m. with his breakfast and a rest to let him digest. He had let his weight catch up with him a bit, so we put him on a *leaning* diet of 35 percent protein, between 50 to 60 percent carbohydrates and from 5 to 8 percent fat. In the morning, he got chicken or turkey salad or some eggs.'

At 10 a.m. Travolta began three hours of intensive jazz-dance training, under the tutelage of Sharee Lane, in an outdoor, tent-topped studio constructed for the workouts. In the 18 weeks before shooting began, he had to learn enough stage-dance technique to make him look like a professional.

After a fish salad for lunch, Travolta began body training at 2 or 2.30 p.m. The sessions would typically start with abdomen work, in which he would do sit-ups on an inclined bench while holding a 30lb weight on his stomach.

Next came free-weight work for the arms, a variety of exercises on the Universal to develop the upper and lower chest, repetitive aerobic exercise in front of a full-length mirror to add definition to specific areas such as the love handles and a few agonising wide-grip pull-ups to broaden the back. 'Many people don't understand that to bring out the chest, they have to work on the back,' Isaacson said adding: 'They work for years just on their chests and wonder why it doesn't develop.'

The one part of Travolta's body Isaacson felt he could ignore was his legs. 'He was getting enough work on them during the dance sessions.'

For the first several weeks of training, Travolta worked to set the base for even more intense work, when weights were increased to develop the muscle to its maximum. During the last two weeks, weights were lessened and repetitions of exercises were increased to bring out the definition of the muscles.

To showcase his new musculature Travolta shaved off most of his body hair and spent time under tanning lights. 'It was all designed so he would peak right at the beginning of filming,' said his trainer.

After a couple of hours of weight training, he and Travolta would run several miles, cooling down with stretches. Dinner, at 6 p.m. consisted of fish or chicken and some vegetables, but very little in the way of dessert. 'John loves chocolate-chip cookies,' said Isaacson explaining, 'but we didn't want him to have sugar. We substituted things sweetened with juice.'

Travolta endured the workouts six days a week for the entire 18-week training period. 'I can't remember John ever missing a day,' said Isaacson. 'John was a good subject for this training. His intensity came from his desire to look the part for the movie.'

The training didn't stop with the shooting of *Staying Alive*. Isaacson and

Travolta kept up the six-days-a-week weight training, even when the only time to train was after midnight. When the production moved to New York to shoot exteriors, Isaacson went along to hold sessions in the hotel gym.

The two planned to open gyms across America to cash in on their hard work. Travolta's screen clothes had spawned plenty of fashion trends: the white polyester three-piece suit, the 50s skinny jeans and leather jackets, the Western outfits, but it wasn't until *Staying Alive* that Travolta decided to endorse his own line of workout wear called Travolta by Carushka. (Carushka Jarecka was the 'in' designer with a multi-million-dollar turnover).

'After every film, I was asked to do clothes. For the first time I felt right about it. It felt much more appropriate to do active-wear than, well, white suits.'

The reception for the clothes and a book *Staying Fit* was better than that for the movie. As suspected and predicted it was The Body not The Actor that was reviewed. Stallone had joked: 'If John keeps this up I'll have to fight him in *Rocky IV* but the battle was with the critics. They saw it as more of a tour of Travolta's torso than a movie. Audiences paid up to see the *Fever* sequel and *Staying Alive* earned respectable millions worldwide but the reaction was more Sunday morning than vibrant Saturday night.

Travolta turned to women. Marilu Henner (who modelled some of the *Staying Fit* book exercises with Travolta) divorced Frederic Forrest in 1983 and with her safely back in his harem, Travolta trumpeted, 'She knows the most intimate things about me. More than my mother or Diana – more than anybody. I trust her more than anyone. This is as serious as I get. She doesn't pressure me. We understand each other. Besides, she finds me really sexy.'

She had also been there during the good and bad times. Travolta's insecurities were mounting and Henner was reassurance and insurance for his happiness.

But he was still driven by the career fever that had separated them all those years before. He had fame and fortune but he wanted peer acceptance. He wanted another Oscar nomination – no, he wanted the Oscars. The praises of Hollywood.

He then – to a degree – disassembled his past. He dissolved his production company, which was headed by Jerry Wurms. Then, more tellingly, he separated – amicably – from Bob Le Mond, who had guided him for a dozen years, explaining, 'Bob and I were in a rut. I just felt I knew what to do if something came up. I began to realise the 80s are all about changing and moving on.

'There were no more discoveries. It was time for independence.'

Chapter Eighteen
The Bubble Bursts

'All they cared about was his body.' Jamie Lee Curtis on Travolta, 1985

With Bob Le Mond out of his career, the anxious Travolta turned to Mike Ovitz who was on his way to becoming the most influential agent in the world. A master of packaging, Ovitz could wrap up multi-million-dollar projects with his stable of directors, producers, writers and actors. It was Ovitz – who also represented Sylvester Stallone – who had dealt the cards that finally added up to *Staying Alive*.

To hell with the critics, Travolta was a box-office champ once more, even if Stallone had crushed his charisma in a vacuum. And that box office had been achieved by staying with what people wanted. It seemed natural for him to re-team with Olivia Newton-John and repeat the partnership which had helped create the most successful movie musical ever.

She had gone on from *Grease* to make *Xanadu*, a movie so bad that when it played on flights on the Los Angeles/New York 'commuter' route it was suggested that passengers were trying to 'leave the theatre at 35,000 feet'. She needed a hit. So did he. 'We'd kept in touch,' said Travolta. 'Several times we had tried to put projects together. Finally *Two of a Kind* came along. I called her and said: "There's a script which has a great role for you and I think even Goldie Hawn would be happy to play. With a couple of changes my part's good too." But I really chose it more for Olivia than myself. I felt it would be very good for her.

'And the best thing was that we were both playing against type – for half of the movie we're quite obnoxious.'

Travolta played a budding inventor, a creator of edible sunglasses and barking doorbells, who decides to become a bank robber. Olivia Newton-John is the flirty bank clerk he confronts and in the gobbledegook that follows they are involved in trying to put the world to rights.

Travolta and Marilu Henner, together with Newton-John and her boyfriend, spent weekends in Santa Barbara relaxing and watching movies – Travolta into the early hours. By then, if he went to bed before 2am he could never sleep. He was truly an 11 p.m. to 2 a.m. man.

Life revolved around Henner, making love, keeping fit and making *Two of a Kind*. Travolta enjoyed the film because first-time director John Herzfeld allowed him to change his lines. 'Over the years some of my biggest arguments have been when I've told a director, "Let me hesitate here, stammer here; let me finish that sentence – that way I'll sound more natural." With John it wasn't like that. There was one scene I couldn't get right. We did it maybe twenty times and finally I changed two words around and it went perfectly. Afterwards he said, "Whenever I let you change a line it works better." '

Clearly, Herzfeld was a candidate for the old Brown Nose Award but Travolta never saw it. *Two of a Kind* was a dog that was soon put out of its misery.

The film-makers had been sure that the mere sight of Travolta and Newton-John together would entrance teenage fans and that the money would roll in. It was all very embarrassing, especially for guest stars like Charles Durning, Beatrice Straight and Scatman Crothers. Admired film critic Peter Rainer, who had hated *Staying Alive*, said of this career dive, 'Travolta had shown surprising versatility but there was still some perception then in critical circles that he was just another overnight hunk. And unfortunately for him his career choices reinforced that perception. He was turning himself into his own caricature.

'It was one of the most distressing spectacles in the movies in those days. He had to work off the tough-tender hood image at an age when most actors are just starting to find the right roles for themselves. He did it and then it all went wrong. Travolta wasn't some Italian Tab Hunter but it's possible he was one of those rare actors who underestimated his talent. What's more likely is that he shocked himself with *Blow Out* – the effect was as raw and visceral as a live encounter – but the public didn't respond so he pulled back to the safety zone. So then we got *Staying Alive* and *Two of A Kind*. It was tragic.'

After rewriting dialogue he was also working on another *Fever* film and there may have been some subliminal thinking in his script: 'I took Tony Manero to Hollywood and put him in MTV rock videos and in movies but things didn't work out and he went back to New York broke and unsuccessful because he had lost his values.' He was also talking to Paramount about directing films; he was a big enough star for them to have found him two properties, a science-fiction thriller and a Howard Hughes film biography, to develop.

At the same time James Bridges was developing a film based on more work from Aaron Latham. Latham's interest had moved from Texas honky-tonks to the LA Sports Connection, a workout empire on Sepulveda Boulevard close to Wilshire

Boulevard – the busiest intersection in the world – where even clients' cars are pampered by valet parking. This land of designer bodies was depicted in Latham's article 'Looking For Mr Goodbody'.

It was – and is – where beautiful people with beautiful bodies connect. Jamie Lee Curtis provided an incredible, jaw-dropping sculpted body as an essential part of her role as the aerobics instructor Jessie, in the imperfect movie *Perfect*. Travolta was the *Rolling Stone* magazine reporter, probing drug dealing and 1980s health-club mating.

All involved saw it as an important film, which would reflect the social mores of the culture. Jamie Lee Curtis complained that it focused more on her crotch than anything else and accused the film-makers of exploitation. She was very aware of the body factor, having witnessed Travolta's drubbing for *Staying Alive*.

'I worked every day with Dan Isaacson and the most important thing I wanted was that it did NOT become like John's did – a total transformation. People stopped looking at his performance and started looking only at his body. All they cared about was his body. His performance was just obliterated by the fact that he changed his body. I was specific that I didn't want to do that. I wanted to look like an athlete. But they went for me – the camera stayed on me too long.

'It was almost pornographic, more pornographic than if it had been naked. If you were nude and making love at least it's…you know! It went on too long. It comes to a point where you either trust the people you're working with or you fight it. I'm not ashamed of it. It does go on a little bit too long. I try to trust people. Everybody says, "Trust me", from the best directors to the worst. I'm the one swivelling my hips in those too-long aerobic scenes.

'John was easy to trust. He's very easygoing, not a tough person to deal with. He's not temperamental or difficult. He doesn't make you feel uncomfortable. He's like that with everyone.

'When we were filming the aerobic class sequences in *Perfect* he would come up and dance on stage for the kids in the class. He would strut and pose – the *Saturday Night Fever* pose and he'd play. He was not afraid to poke fun at himself and have a good time.

'John is the movie star. In terms of lifestyle he always has been. He loves being a movie star. He makes no bones about it.'

By the time he filmed *Perfect* in 1985 this particular movie star was certified to fly seven different types of jets. He had bought a 550 m.p.h. Lockheed JetStar 731 some months earlier and had logged two hundred hours in it flying to Britain, Greece, Egypt (where he was greeted by two thousand fans) and France. He also owned a Cessna Citation and a Constellation. At the ranch there was a high-powered stable of machinery: a Jaguar XJ6, a 1964 Rolls-Royce, a Mercedes and Cadillac and that classic yellow Thunderbird.

'There's an innate sense of glamour about John,' said James Bridges.

Also, a certain style. When he had been under pressure working with Bridges on *Urban Cowboy* a young actress had auditioned. Rene Russo remembered: 'Years ago when I read with him for *Urban Cowboy* it was my first screen test. I'll never forget how lovely and supportive he was. He said: "You really have something." I could tell he was sincere.'

And a *star*. He and Marilu Henner had gone off on what she called 'passion-choked' trips and had taken a chartered yacht around the French West Indies. They were together in *Perfect*: she was one of the aerobics club members in a secondary storyline but each day she and the leading man woke up together in their suite at the Westwood Marquis Hotel. In the evenings they'd wander around the Los Angeles university area cafes and shops, and at weekends it was off to Santa Barbara.

As *Perfect* opened in American cinemas Travolta was having doubts about keeping the ranch. The critics loathed it. Many hated him playing a reporter.

'John certainly didn't come out of the picture back where he was,' said James Bridges. It wasn't for want of trying. As he has always done he went out to 'sell' the film with promotional appearances and interviews. Often his efforts were thrown back at him. He would be asked about his body hair in *Staying Alive* (it had come off with Nair cream after body waxing 'hurt like a mother') and his body in *Perfect* ('I take an aerobic class but I'm wearing a big sweatshirt') and the black bikini underwear in *Saturday Night Fever*. There were lots of body shots in *Perfect* including some of model-actor Paul Barresi.

During the *Perfect* promotions there was much talk about Travolta's sex life, including this question: 'Does it bother you that there are men who claim they've had sex with you?' He replied:

'Actually, there is this one *girl* who is fairly famous who said, "Oh, yeah, I had sex with John." I've never had anything with her. It's par for the course. But I guess if you told me a name I could probably call them up and say, "Did you say that?" And then I would probably call you up. Or maybe get you both on the phone.'

He had celebrated his thirtieth birthday with a small party at the ranch – he flew his sister Margaret and her family in from Chicago – and this turning point appeared to find him more relaxed. 'I know now that one movie isn't going to make all the difference for me. Believe me, that's settled me down a lot.'

Even so, Travolta was a multi-million-dollar leading man in need of a box-office success but he was still very much the star and found himself with an invitation to the Reagan White House for a dinner-dance honouring Prince Charles and Princess Diana. Princess Diana had asked for him to be present, along with Clint Eastwood, who was then running for Mayor of the Californian coastal resort of Carmel, Tom Selleck, who was then a huge favourite with his series *Magnum PI*, and songmaster Neil Diamond.

Awed by Eastwood, the star-struck Princess appeared more relaxed with Travolta who – primed by First Lady Nancy Reagan – asked her to dance. As Neil Diamond belted out a couple of uptempo hits she got her wish and was whisked expertly around the floor by Travolta. The perfect gentleman with charisma in overdrive, he enjoyed the royal connection. As he and everyone around him says, he *enjoys* being a star.

'My theory is if I saw a star resentful of what he has I'd say, "How dare he?" God, if somebody is not going to live it to the fullest why did they want it? Growing up, if I had thought Warren Beatty and Faye Dunaway in *Bonnie and Clyde* didn't jet around and dress up and meet royalty and have fine things it would have *killed* me.'

Travolta had all these things. What he didn't have was a hit movie or, he felt, the artistic respect he deserved. It was the beginning of his eclipse. He regarded *Perfect* as the party he had thrown that nobody came to.

After all the hard work, he was bitter and frustrated and he considered taking to the skies forever – as an airline pilot. 'I thought, wouldn't it be wild to give up this career and then be going, "Hello, this is your captain, John Travolta."

'I didn't think my career was over but I thought that I might not want it anymore. I didn't know if I could take the whole package. Was it worth the pleasure of making a movie – which is always a pleasure – and the pain of releasing it? I remember saying to someone at the time, "I don't know if I can continue doing this."

'I was sort of feeling out of it and then two wonderful things happened. Whoopi Goldberg wanted to make a movie with me and she was the hottest thing going following *The Colour Purple*. And Princess Di had wanted to dance with me.

'And I thought, "Even when things are bad they are pretty damn good." '

He had danced with Diana but didn't get to act with Whoopi Goldberg even after a year spent developing a comedy for Cannon Films. 'We could never get the script right and finally Whoopi had to go back to work.'

So did he – in something completely different. Everything was changing. The Santa Barbara ranch, his hacienda bolt-hole in the high hills, had been sold by the Sears Realty Company in Montecito for close to the asking price of $3.9 million dollars and he had linked up with Jonathan Krane as his new manager. Bob Le Mond, his link with the past, had died. Le Mond had suffered from AIDS for some time and Travolta had been a constant visitor to his bedside. He had been to see him only two days before his death in the first week of September 1986. Lois Zetter had moved to Las Vegas. They saw each other at Le Mond's funeral.

Travolta found comfort with another 'family' – Kirstie Alley and her husband Parker Stevenson. The *Cheers* actress and her easygoing husband (a one-time television *Hardy Boy*, he grew up to be on *Baywatch*) had their own 'family' of animals. They live in Encino just down the street from Michael Jackson's Los Angeles home. The 'hot' weekend activity is skateboarding down the drive or taking dinky, electric cars for a spin. They shared the fun and in Kirstie Alley the burned-out Travolta found a fellow Scientology devotee. He liked her – even if she insists on organic food.

He was doing more flying than working and his disillusionment with Hollywood and California led him to search for a home in Florida. He was also on the lookout for work and the combination of two names – Harold Pinter and Robert Altman – had him excited. Altman, director of film classics like *M*A*S*H*, *Nashville* and *The Player*, had considered Bob Hoskins and David Bowie for a television production of Pinter's *The Dumbwaiter*.

Gary Pudney, vice president and senior executive in charge of specials for ABC, had approached Altman to see if he had any ideas for television plays. Altman recalls, 'I had tried to sell the idea to HBO but Pinter was too esoteric for them. So, I was shocked that a network was willing to do it. I think Pudney was alone at ABC in wanting to try this. Everybody thought he was crazy, but he pushed it through. He looked on it as a way of going back to the golden age of television.'

It was Pudney who suggested casting Travolta in the the lead in the story of two gunman falling apart, but Tom Conti, the Scots actor, had already been offered the role. Pudney had been an ABC executive when Travolta played Vinnie Barbarino. The two had remained friends and he said: 'For years I'd been looking for something to bring John back to television. Originally, I was thinking of him for something musical, but when Altman suggested *The Dumbwaiter* I thought of John. I have to admit that Altman gave me a rather sceptical look when I mentioned his name. But I set up a lunch, and they got along famously. Altman offered Travolta the second lead explaining, 'I was quite taken with him. I had to know he really wanted to do it. He didn't do it for the money because I didn't pay him much.'

Travolta had reservations about returning to television; he knew that the industry often interprets such a move as a career comedown and a clear sign of a performer's desperation. 'Every year Gary Pudney called me about doing something for television and I'd be very polite and back off. When he told me to come to his office I thought, "How am I going to get out of it this time?" But when he mentioned Altman and Pinter, I couldn't believe it.'

Before his lunch with Altman at Manhattan's luvvie restaurant, the Russian Tea

Room, he studied the play and practised a Cockney accent. While they were eating he launched into some dialogue. 'He really loved the idea that I would do that just for fun. Frankly, I don't know how familiar Altman was with my work before then. I really think it was my performing at the Russian Tea Room that made him think I could do the part.

'I know why people work for Altman for nothing. It's because he gives you an adventure as an actor. His key is that he gives you seeds to work with.' Travolta says he was not trying to prove anything by tackling Pinter. 'Any smart actor would do something like that regardless of when it came up. But I think it was more fun because I hadn't worked in so long and had all that energy to give to the project.' He went on to admit: 'I was burned out. If I had been told I would never have to work again I would have said "great". I finally calmed down.'

But the critics had been hard. And they were again with headlines like, 'Travolta Fails In Try At Classic Role'. He seemed to give an emotional, philosophical shrug. 'The main concern you have after a failure is your survival. Are there still offers? Are you going to go back to work? As long as offers are still there, you can get through it.'

He thought about that and added, 'Sometimes when you explore it's hard to find your way back to the trail.'

Since he had starred in *Perfect* nothing had led in the right direction and now stories were beginning to appear with the headline: Whatever happened to…

Chapter Nineteen
You Talking To Me?

'I don't play violins for myself.'

John Travolta, 1989

Travolta was in a tailspin. He had gone from high-stepping to mis-stepping and he knew it but, confronted with what appeared an impossible career situation, he charged back in the Hollywood 'house' newspaper, the *Los Angeles Times*.

It was his first interview since *Perfect* had flopped. Pat Broeske, one of the paper's most insightful showbusiness writers, described him as retaining 'a star's pride as well as a star's charisma'. She pointed out that he did not want to acknowledge that his career had gone off track. To emphasise her argument she explained how Travolta had turned down the chance to co-present with Olivia Newton-John the 1989 Oscar for Best Music Score. In 1978, the year he was first nominated he had presented the Best Supporting Actress Oscar to Vanessa Redgrave for *Julia*. Three years later he handed Barbra Streisand her honorary Oscar. A year later it was another big one, the Best Actor award to Ben Kingsley for *Gandhi*.

Travolta explained to her: 'I felt I had some kind of stat there.' But stature in Hollywood gets chipped away quickly. 'Just as he was glorified for his successes he was blamed for his failures,' wrote Broeske.

Travolta wasn't having it. 'Whatever you do you shouldn't depict me as a victim, because if you depict me as one you'll be wrong. I don't feel like a victim. I don't play violins for myself. I never have.'

He signed on to make *The Experts* which was about a couple of guys who weren't – at anything. He co-starred with Ayre Gross in the $13 million Paramount film as a *Dumb and Dumber* style pair who find themselves trying to teach Soviet spies about contemporary America. Actress Kelly Preston – the future Mrs Travolta – played an engaging and rather warm Iron Curtain warrior.

The film was shown in some cinemas in Oklahoma and Texas and Colorado. One critic said he thought Travolta was dead. Another wrote simply, 'Blaaaah!!!' Travolta said: 'Everyone's asking what happened. I wish I had ten bucks for every time I've heard that.' Kicked when you're down? He was being run over.

He wouldn't have it. 'I don't blame anybody for anything in my life. I don't like blame, shame or regret. What's the point? Hey, you try turning the clock back. It doesn't matter what people think about me. They can say what they want. But the fact is they've never been where I've been.'

Suddenly every other movie looked like a potential Travolta vehicle but he either wasn't being considered for them or rejected them. He saw potential in *The Tender*, a $10 million movie being co-produced by hitmaking star Michael Douglas. It starred Travolta as a desperate alcoholic who, together with his daughter, finds a wounded dog and a way to save their relationship. The tale is wagged by the dog: the story is told through its eyes. In some video stores the movie appeared as *Eyes of an Angel*.

Then it was suggested he might star in a remake of *Zorba the Greek*, but that idea sank without a trace.

By now, Travolta's love of food was showing. With no pun intended he said, 'I'm fairly big on eating. And I don't like exercise. When I am happy or when I am miserable I love to eat. Nothing puts me off my food. On my deathbed I will be yelling, "Gimme another slice!!." ' He weighed more than 200lbs (fifteen stone) when he filmed *The Tender* but he dropped some weight before filming *Chains of Gold*.

With Jonathan Krane and the backing of Krane's Management Company Entertainment Group (MCEG) it looked as though *Chains of Gold* with Travolta as a do-good hero battling drug dealers for the future of a young boy would soar, especially outside America. Again Marilu Henner was there for support and in the movie Travolta had a love scene with her, shirtless. There were love handles on the lean machine of *Staying Alive*.

He was aware of the weight but strangely ambivalent about it saying: 'I don't know what audiences will think.' Unfortunately, there were no audiences and, like *The Experts* and *The Tender* one of the few slim elements about *Chains of Gold* was its budget. Off-screen Travolta was still the star. With the Santa Barbara ranch sold he invested in a fly-in country club family community in Florida. Spruce Creek is five miles from Daytona Beach and has room for 320 planes. He moved his white Lear jet into a French provincial airplane hangar and himself into a four-bedroom, four-bathroom grey and white French provincial home. It was paradise for him: he could literally fly his plane into the 'garage' and open a door to his living room.

'He fitted right in,' said Spruce Creek developer Jay Thompson. 'He's such a nice person, low-key and unpretentious. He was very visible in the community and people took him for granted.'

That was until he wanted to drop in with his Gulfstream 11 jet, which is the size of a small commercial airliner and weighs 62,000lbs fully loaded. The governing board of the flying community ruled it was too big and too noisy for Spruce Creek.

Travolta was devastated. He appealed against the decision and won the first round but the controversy upset him.

California – Hollywood, really – was a long way off. He explained, 'I think you have to be as strong as Streisand or Stallone to stay in that town. You have to have nerves of steel. I'm not like that. I'm strong in character but I don't like the fight. *I don't like the fight.*'

His friend Kirstie Alley was talking about a film titled *Daddy's Home*. She was so popular in *Cheers* that Tri-Star Pictures saw it as a vehicle for her. It had been written and was to be directed by Amy Heckerling who had made her mark with *Fast Times at Ridgemount High* in 1982.

Alley would be a pregnant thirtysomething and the action would be led by her baby Mickey, who wants a father. The new title *Look Who's Talking* said it all. With Bruce Willis as the voice of the miniature matchmaker, Tri-Star and producer Jonathan Krane had a package. Travolta was to be the cab driver who Mickey decides will be his dad. The movie runs for thirty minutes before a tubby Travolta appears.

Within four weeks *Look Who's Talking* had taken $50 million. For Hollywood money talks. And Travolta's latest went on doing just that.

Travolta, bewildered but delighted, found himself in his first hit for a long time. The film-makers were a little wary of that. Everybody had an explanation for the movie's success but his name didn't come up a lot. Amy Heckerling said, 'I have this theory that people are embarrassed about anything they liked in the 1970s. I think people hold their hatred of discos against John. And for bell bottoms. And the rest of the fads. But the fact is John's not responsible for what we all did during that decade.'

Travolta was delighted for Kirstie Alley and warily, gauchely admitted, 'Golly, it's nice to have a success again.'

It was. He and Marilu Henner had settled into a platonic phase. She was seeing director/producer Rob Lieberman and Travolta had a new girl but publicly he was keeping quiet about her identity other than saying, 'She's sorta famous.' Of Henner his 'forever friend' he said, 'We're finally settling into the idea that we're friends, that it's not a problem just to be friends. You always feel that attraction to someone. It is hard to turn it off but you do it out of morals, respect and ethics. You have to.'

He also had to take on *Look Who's Talking Too* in 1990, with the addition of Roseanne Barr's voice, and *Look Who's Talking Now*, the 1993 follow-up which focused on the marriage and comfortable performances of Alley and Travolta. Between these two Travolta squeezed in two clunkers. *Boris and Natasha*, directed in 1991 by Charlie Williams Smith, who had been so memorable in Brian De Palma's *The Untouchables* in 1989, was never released in cinemas unlike 1992's

Shout with Travolta as a music teacher on-the-run, but mercifully its outing was short-lived.

Look Who's Talking had re-established Travolta's celebrity but not his credibility. It was regarded as luck rather than judgement after all the awful career choices of the past. 'Everyone at the time said, "He's back." Then, all of a sudden, he wasn't back,' said *Phenomenon* director Jon Turteltaub.

Travolta knew all about dispensability ('even at the height of my career I was dispensable') but he had the money. And he also had Kelly Preston. He reflected in 1996 that he had been in 'a cynical black hole where I could hardly function'. He came out of it mostly because of Preston. She was born Kelly Palzis in Honolulu on 13 October 1963. She has lived a nomad life, having travelled and lived with her parents in Iraq, Australia and finally California where she attended two universities before graduation to daytime soaps, prime-time television and the movies. She appeared as a nude model with Ann-Margret and Roy Scheider in an adaption of Elmore Leonard's *52 Pick-Up* in 1985 and 'deflowered' a gleefully-innocent Arnold Schwarzenegger in *Twins* in 1988.

Just as she was filming her first kiss with the big man his wife, newscaster Maria Shriver, turned up on the set. 'I went over and introduced myself because sometimes *I* feel a bit awkward when someone is kissing on your man. And I was in the tiniest postage-stamp dress.'

Three years before *Twins* she had married actor Kevin Gage, who co-starred with her when she played a teenage astronaut in *Space Camp*. After two difficult years it ended in divorce and she became involved with actor George Clooney, whom she had first met in acting class in 1985.

Clooney, who played the boss in *Roseanne* before moving on to *E.R.* and Quentin Tarantino's 1996 bullets-and-fangs epic *From Dusk Till Dawn*, wasn't a big spender on their first date. They went to Hobson's Ice Cream Parlour in Los Angeles. Within a month they had bought a house together which they shared with Max, Clooney's pet pig. Within a year they had separated and – Hollywood is a small town – she began going out with Charlie Sheen who had co-starred with Clooney in the 1984 clunker *Grizzly II – The Predator*.

Sheen, who later gave evidence against convicted Hollywood madam Heidi Fleiss, saying he had spent $50,000 on her girls, has a wild reputation. His affair with Preston revolved around a chunky 25-carat, $200,000 diamond engagement ring and a startling incident with a gun.

In mid-January 1990 she was taken to hospital with injuries to her right wrist and ankle. Sheen's handgun had accidentally gone off in her apartment in the Maison de Ville complex in Malibu. Preston told police she was alone in her bedroom when the gun dropped on the floor and discharged. Sheen, she said, was in another part of the home. After treatment at Santa Monica Hospital she was released. Small pieces of porcelain were removed from her wounds. All Preston said of the incident was through her then spokesperson Jeff Ballard who offered a crisp, 'It was an accident.'

The Preston/Sheen romance engaged Hollywood gossips most of all when they broke up. Did she keep the ring? Preston finally settled all the talk by explaining that they had sold the ring and split the proceeds.

Travolta told the story of how he and Kelly got together. 'Kelly is maybe the most beautiful girl in the world and very few people will argue the point. I met her on *The Experts*. We became friends in a three-month period and I fell in love with her but she was married. It was at the end of the movie at the wrap party that I knew I was in love with her. I wanted someone who would never leave my side. I wanted that kind of commitment and I knew she was the one for me but I couldn't tell her that – not then.

'Her marriage was a precarious thing but we were very clean in our interplay with each other. We were above board but I knew that was when I first loved her. I helped her with some techniques of Scientology; she was open-minded about it. She liked to travel and she didn't mind flying. She liked to dance and she liked to eat. It was so refreshing but she was married. It was too bad.'

During his solitary life in Florida he turned up in Los Angeles for a business meeting, which coincided with a gathering at Parker Stevenson and Kirstie Alley's house in Encino. Alley played matchmaker. Preston was still seeing Charlie Sheen but Alley told her and Travolta: 'Why don't you two get together?'

Later in Vancouver while she was filming the Disney action film *Run* and he was there on location with *Look Who's Talking Too* they met up again. By then Sheen was history. 'He asked if I was over Charlie and I was,' recalls Preston. 'When we'd first met I developed a bit of a crush on him but it was actually more of a professional relationship with a little bit of a crush in there. But... but I have this story: 'When I was fifteen and living with my family in Australia we went to see *Grease*. Before we walked into the cinema I saw this poster and I had this flash that I was going to be with this man in the future. I'd already seen *Saturday Night Fever*. At that time disco was a huge craze in Australia. My mom and I went to disco class with about two hundred other women. I kept telling the instructor I was going to marry that man in the movie. I didn't really remember it until John asked me to go out and then I said, "Oh, God..." ' '

Which was tame compared with what Paul Barresi had to say. He claimed Travolta picked him up in a Los Angeles health club shower room and they were involved in a homosexual relationship.

Barresi said they started an affair that night in 1982 and Travolta paid him the going rate for a day's work in the porn movie, $440, each time they got together. He alleged he and Travolta had sex "dozens of times" over two years, while Travolta was involved with Winger, Olivia Newton-John and Marilu Henner – and he once had Barresi leave a Hawaiian love nest just before Henner's arrival. Barresi said Travolta often talked about the trio of stars while in bed with him.

He claimed Travolta liked to listen to lurid details of Barresi's sexual conquests. In an interview published in 1990 in the *National Enquirer* the model-actor said: 'John used to call me his *Midnight Cowboy*. He told me again and again that I was sexier and more macho than Burt Reynolds and Clark Gable combined.

'There were times I thought, "I wonder what John's millions of female fans would think if they could see the two of us together." John was bisexual but it never seemed to bother him that his sexual behaviour with me was a shocking contrast to his big–screen image.'

Barresi's story was utterly denied by Travolta's public relations representatives Travolta issued a formal denial of Barresi's claims through his press representatives, which was seen as enough for claims that were regarded with disdain.

More pertinent were the thoughts of director James Bridges, one of the few who was certain that a Travolta resurrection was about to happen. His crystal ball just didn't reflect the correct vehicle: 'You know what I'd like. I'd like to do a second *Saturday Night Fever* sequel.

'I'd bring John's character to Hollywood and have his story parallel what's happened to John.

'But – we would have a happy ending.'

Chapter Twenty
Married Man

'Showbusiness has no memory.' Lois Zetter, 1989

B y 1996 Kelly Preston was a mother and had reached level 12 in Scientology. She was full of *Beingness*, *Doingness* and *Havingness* and was brimming with confidence for the future.

Appropriately, love and marriage for Travolta had gone at a jet pace. Travolta – an 'Operating Thetan' in Scientology – is a man of expensive, impressive impulse. He'd fly Preston off for meals and love in the sky. On New Year's Eve 1990, he had gathered family and friends around them at the Palace Hotel in Gstaad, Switzerland. 'Earlier in the day I'd passed by a jewellery store and seen the most beautiful ring and said to myself, "You're going to propose in six months anyway, why not get the ring now?" ' He did but did not have six months of patience. 'That night I shocked the heck out of everyone.'

Jonathan Krane was with his wife Sally Kellerman at the table. 'When John proposed Kelly screamed.'

When would they marry? The engagement ran a soap-opera path. He dithered. She sulked. He sulked. She dithered. But he knew: 'Kelly is the person who would never leave my side. I know it. I guess I had my opportunity to be married to some of the greatest women on the planet but there was always something different about Kelly, a quality that reminded me of Diana Hyland in a way. When we got back together that's when I hung my hat up.

'I've lost lots of people that I love but I learned that when it comes to loving people you don't really have a choice. If you want to feel alive and experience something wonderful you have to risk great loss. Relationships mean too much to me now to ever walk away.'

But they almost didn't walk down the aisle. One set of marriage plans were cancelled and then Travolta in a *Casablanca* mood decided they would 'always have Paris'. It was after a dinner at Spruce Creek that Preston announced to a jaw-dropped Travolta that he was going to be a father. 'I never expected the news. I was walking on air. I still am. This was everything I wanted.'

He had everything – except a home for more than parking a plane. And, of course, a wedding ceremony. He wanted a house on the East Coast, a hideaway where a child could have an Ivy League upbringing. Kirstie Alley had a home in Maine and he bought a twenty-room stone mansion on the coast just five miles from her. It had been built in 1899 by a Philadelphia tycoon and had turrets, gables and spectacular sea views. Winters are still spent at the 'down to earth place' in Florida and also at a hideaway home near Carmel in California. Maine ('I feel like I'm in *my* novel') is for summer living – and Christmas, when the Travolta clan gathers, usually more than fifty of them, to celebrate with 'the brat'.

Kelly Preston is a very welcome clan member.

A Scientology minister flown from Florida married them on 5 September 1991, at the Hotel de Crillon in Paris. Hotel staff were not told of the marriage in the second-floor private dining room until 4 p.m. when a three-tier wedding cake was ordered. It was all part of the secrecy.

Travolta wore a tuxedo and his bride a white, low-cut bridal gown. Her curls cascaded over her shoulders and there were tears in her eyes when they married at midnight in a twenty-minute ceremony. Banquet manager Bertrand Heintz recalled, 'The room was crammed with flowers and a violinist played the "Wedding March"; it was so romantic.'

Not so romantic were the technical problems. The marriage was not registered with French authorities, which made its validity questionable. Travolta, the star, had to stage a press conference to make it clear that they were married. A civil ceremony in Florida cleared up any dangling legalities.

Kelly Preston had no doubt that she was Mrs John Travolta. And wanted to be. 'The way he swept me off my feet took my breath away. John is the most wonderful kisser and has the most gentle manner. I just melted.

'He's one of the world's greatest lovers and made me feel I was the only woman on earth. I fell in love with him during a matter of days. I already knew he had a fantastic personality and was kind but he knew how to give incredible pleasure. He's the world's most romantic man who is never pushy, forceful or crude.

'I now know he'll only go ahead when he's absolutely sure his love will be returned. Like me, he'd been hurt – and was very cautious and wary. He'd always been guarded about his love life because he felt it tacky to discuss his intimate private life.

'This led to all sorts of false rumours like him being gay. He just shrugged it off in the same way he deals with everything. He knew the truth for himself and didn't have to explain to anybody.'

Before their romance she admitted thinking, 'Here was a famous man in his late thirties and unmarried. I wondered about his quiet, charming approach and thought perhaps he was a committed bachelor.' No more. 'I was crazy about this man and that's the way it's stayed. He was so definite about what he wanted – a family and marriage.

'I was pregnant after the very first time we tried to make a baby. We were staying with our good friends Demi Moore and Bruce Willis. I could hardly believe the whole thing happened so fast.

'I started that year regarding John as just a friend and now I was madly in love with the guy and expecting his baby. I feel as if I'm married to Superman. Charlie Sheen is a real Hollywood player and everything has to be about him. John's such a contrast – unselfish and caring and whatever work he's doing he does not want us to be apart.'

Indeed, during her pregnancy Travolta was eating for three. It showed. He says he couldn't have cared less.

Jett Travolta was born weighing 8lb, 12oz, at 12.33 a.m. on 13 April 1992, in virtual silence at Daytona Beach Hospital in a birthing method advocated by Scientology founder L. Ron Hubbard. He was named not just because of his father's love of flying but also as a combination of his father's and godmother Ellen Travolta's initials. Jett was the only one roaring at his birth.

'There is a lot of pain going on so the idea is you don't want to add to the pain by adding verbal statements because they're recorded in the mind of the baby. Later, that could cause certain kinds of fears or neuroses or even psychosomatic illnesses,' said Travolta:

'Even if the mother were to injure herself during the pregnancy she should keep quiet. She should keep quiet even if she sneezes. You have to take care of women during pregnancy and during birthing because everything that happens to them is a reflection of what's going to happen in our future. You can't help but have respect for women, what they are capable of doing, what they go through, the pain they endure and then the gift that they give to life.

'I never loved Kelly as much as I did watching her give birth to Jett. It's a new chapter in your emotional life – it's just something that comes over you like a wave. After he was born and cleaned up I held him for hours while Kelly slept. When they came to take him away for tests I said they couldn't see him that day. I went a little nutsy.

'The love affair she's having with my son thrills me no end because it makes him so happy. Kelly does a lot of things for me. She loves me and I *know* she loves me. She has a commitment to me that I believe in my heart is for a lifetime – she's not going anywhere – and I like that. It makes me feel good. I have a feeling of stability with her. I think anything could happen and we could work it out.

'The first two years of his life I got to spend a lot of time with him but lately I've been the working dad again. Kelly's made up for that. I know he's with Mom so everything is fine.'

The circle of life. Mom and the baby. That's exactly how it had been for Travolta but now he was *the* man not just of the house but Hollywood.

Quentin Tarantino had struggled to be allowed to cast Travolta as Vincent Vega – not just against Miramax Films but against Travolta himself. Finally, after hours spent with Tarantino, he agreed and said, 'I felt if I'm gonna play someone as *bold* as this heroin hit man I'd better do it in good company with a *great* script and *great* director.

'Quentin, who believed in me as an actor, gave me the stellar opportunity. I was working on the third of the *Look Who's Talking* movies, which I was doing to keep alive in showbusiness when I got a call.

'It was like this young man comes into my life and gives me an opportunity to rekindle the kind of career people expected from me and that I expected from myself. There was always a trickle of hope brought in with each production but in 1993 I just decided to live my life and stop worrying about my career. Then, within a couple of days, I got a call from Quentin.'

The flashback here is to the Four Seasons Hotel at the smart end of Doheny Drive near Wilshire Boulevard in Beverly Hills. Through the elegant bar and into the restaurant Tarantino, nearly a dozen years younger than his lunch guest, sat at a window table with Travolta.

'In the back of my mind I hoped we'd get along and that I could work with him later,' recalled Tarantino. 'I just wanted to *meet* him.' Travolta only went to the lunch at the urging of Jonathan Krane and because of Tarantino's enthusiasm. He had watched *Reservoir Dogs*, the film that had made Tarantino's name, on video and wondered, Would I be in something like this?

Emma Thompson was at a nearby table. She wandered over to flatter Travolta. She had been a fan since her uncle took her to see *Saturday Night Fever*. Then she turned to Tarantino and commanded, 'Put this man in one of your movies. He needs a good movie.'

Tarantino provided it. Later it prompted his star to muse, 'I have a theory. When people refer to a comeback it doesn't mean you didn't work. It means that you weren't in a film that registered. It's like, "Oh, you think I haven't been doing anything? Well, does that mean the last ten years of my life just disappeared?" '

A huge Travolta fan, Tarantino won his case to place him in a eclectic but enviable group including Sam L. Jackson, Christopher Walken, Bruce Willis, Uma Thurman,

Eric Stoltz, Rosanna Arquette, Harvey Keitel, Tim Roth and Amanda Plummer. The cast alone would have bust Tarantino's budget of $8 million. They – not just Travolta – worked for small financial returns. 'It was an act of love.' said Travolta.

It was also, of course, the best bet he had. And for once in a long time he played it perfectly.

It cost Travolta $30,000 of his $140,000 fee to have his wife and son with him during filming but he would have paid Tarantino for the chance to be in the movie. 'He gave me my hat back as an artist. I felt the same way about doing *The Dumbwaiter* with Altman. There are movies that you make to keep your integrity as an actor.' What he found out from *Pulp Fiction* is that he still had the magic – and that hard man and Martin Scorsese-graduate, Harvey Keitel, liked *Grease*.

A strange world.

Travolta's trick was to turn the paunchy and monstrous Vincent Vega into a likeable killer; Vega became more black comedy than *film noir*.

He considered all the social implications. He had been a trendsetter from disco to country and western. He knew the power of the movies. He did not want to advocate heroin addiction. 'I had influenced people but what I came up with was: "You mess with drugs, you die. You mess with murder, you die". Everybody's headed for death in this piece. We were not glorifying violence.'

Some scenes are already part of film buff legend: the discussion between Vega and Bible-and-people-thumping colleague Jules played by Sam Jackson about what the French call a McDonald's hamburger; the moment when Uma Thurman overdoses; and the dance.

Travolta is squeezed into partnering Thurman's gorgeous gangland moll in a dance contest at Jack Rabbit Slim's diner, which is a heaven – or hell – of waiters looking like Buddy Holly, Marilyn Monroe, Elvis and a string of other American 50s faces. But the dance is the thing. Vega is making shuffling heroin hops with Thurman, following the dance dare from Ed Sullivan lookalike Jerry Hoban. Then the V-sign from his childhood twisting comes into play. Dressed to kill – they are both in Agnes B: she in a white shirt and black cigarette pants and he in the black suit with the leather collar – they do 'The Swim' to Chuck Berry's 'You Never Can Tell'.

Uma Thurman was lost at first. 'Quentin had a clear idea about it and John knew the dances. I didn't know "The Swim" or "The Batman" and "The Catwoman". John was an expert. He made it all happen.'

She was with Travolta, Sam L. Jackson, Bruce Willis and Tarantino when *Pulp Fiction* was screened in competition at the Cannes Film Festival in May 1994. Before it had won the Palme d'Or the French Riviera was buzzing about the movie, about Tarantino and most of all about Travolta.

It was open adulation season. A group of German journalists asked Travolta how it felt to have been a star and then been fat and made flops. He could laugh and tell them, 'I was thin then.'

Now, he could be as fat as he pleased. It was raves all the way. Uma Thurman remembered, 'John was nearly in tears.'

Later, Travolta would often repeat how he had to leave company to deal with his emotions. 'I felt not only that the film was being celebrated but that *I* was being celebrated. That was very moving. I'd be a bullshit artist to say it wasn't.'

There was much of that particular commodity flying around *Pulp Fiction*. And quite rightly. All involved had taken a chance and the high risks justified the similar awards. It was a *Pulp Fiction* love fest between Travolta and Tarantino. At Cannes all the praise was being stacked on Tarantino for Travolta's 'comeback' turn and he replied, 'Giving me credit for John's performance is like telling me I have a beautiful wife; what did I have to do with it? '

Travolta liked that. 'See what integrity he has? You know what he said later, "Now, if you give me credit for for choosing John then I'll take that as a compliment." ' And then there was:

'When I said to to him, "Quentin, you've got everybody to love me again," he said, "They always loved you John and I just gave them permission. " '

The Oscar nominations came in.

Sam Jackson was a 1995 Best Supporting Actor Oscar nominee for Jules Winnfield, the Bible-quoting (Ezekiel 25:17) hit man and one of cinema's everlasting characters. Ironically he says he was so confident that he had the role he almost lost it. The script had been tailored around him. He *was* Jules. But he admits he did not prepare as he normally would for a reading of the role. 'I didn't do any of the things that as an actor I automatically would go through. I just expected it to be mine. I was too relaxed. Another actor had a shot at it – I went berserk. I had my manager and my agent calling everyone.

'Later, thank God, I got another chance and I worked and worked before it. And I kicked ass at that audition. I tell you I now take nothing for granted. Nothing is ever handed to you. Sometimes you get seduced into thinking that happens but it really doesn't. I almost lost the role of a lifetime by being too confident. I won't take that sort of risk again.

'It's something John and I talked about. He understands that situation so well.'

Travolta was nominated as Best Actor for the second time. The competition was Nigel Hawthorne for *The Madness of King George*, Paul Newman for *Nobody's Fool*, Morgan Freeman for *The Shankshaw Redemption* and Travolta's longtime friend Tom Hanks for *Forrest Gump*.

Tarantino and writer Roger Avary received an Academy Award nomination for Best Screenplay and on 27 March 1995, at the Dorothy Chandler Pavilion they collected the award, which was announced by Sir Anthony Hopkins. Sam Jackson stayed in his seat as Martin Landau accepted his Best Supporting Actor for his role as horror star Bela Lugosi in *Ed Wood*.

Travolta also stayed seated as Tom Hanks took the Best Actor Oscar in an awards sweep by *Forrest Gump*.

It hurt, but he consoled himself.

Didn't everybody love him again?

Chapter Twenty One
Get Travolta

'I remembered *Look Who's Talking* and thought: "Oh, no, Jesus... not Travolta." ' author Elmore Leonard, 1996

Elmore Leonard is the Dickens from Detroit who writes what he calls 'crime thrillers' involving strangely principled hoodlums, whores, conmen and hustlers. His wonderful underworld is a Grand National of zanies and wackos chasing a winner but usually finding there are too many hurdles. He has a Panasonic ear for real life dialogue and a penchant for black and stag humour. ('When the girls would say do-it-to-me, do-it-to-me, he would think: What do you think I'm doing?')

Elmore Leonard, in his Kangol cap and wispy beard looks more like an absent-minded professor. He was 70 in 1996. And to his fans he has been the master of ten-minute-boiled fiction for years. Many of his books have been filmed while others slipped through the endless Tinseltown meetings and negotiations.

That's how *Get Shorty* became a John Travolta vehicle – it is Leonard's revenge on Hollywood. A spectacular one as it turned out.

When Leonard's *La Brava* was published he was approached by the formidable team of director Martin Scorsese and the actor Dustin Hoffman who wanted to film it. Leonard's agent told him the film would never be made. He was right. Instead, *Get Shorty*, the story of the debacle, was written.

And Leonard beat Hollywood again. Danny DeVito whose company Jersey Films had co-produced *Pulp Fiction*, received a phone call in his car from associate Barry Sonnenfeld. DeVito was about to take a plane trip. 'Buy the new Leonard book *Get Shorty*,' urged Sonnenfeld.

He intended DeVito to have an enjoyable read on the plane trip from Los Angeles to New York. Instead, DeVito bought the movie rights to the book and rang his associate back: 'Hey, Barry, we got it. We own the book.'

Sonnenfeld: 'That's great. What'd you think of the book?'

DeVito: 'I haven't read it.'

Travolta had. Like most people he adored it. It's a pertinent mirror of Elmore

Leonard's junk souls world where even participles are pared. Martin Amis scored when he said that in Leonard's thrillers, 'Death roams the land disguised as money'.

Elmore Leonard is a nine-to-five man. Generally each day he sits at his 200-year old desk writing in longhand (he revises on a reconditioned portable typewriter) without a break for lunch at the home he shares with his second wife Joan. It is fifteen miles outside Detroit but even further away from the streets his characters prowl. He has created a memorable rainbow of tough, evil, sad, sadistic, sometimes sympathetic but best of all just plain psycho-crazy characters.

His owlish appearance is deceiving. He provides material for those who want to read fast, often absurdly funny, occasionally violent, sometimes sexy page-turners. The critics put him in hallowed sentences with Dashiel Hammett, Raymond Chandler and Ross McDonald and he does not complain about that company. It's just not quite accurate. They wrote mysteries. He writes thrillers.

He talks softly. 'The puzzle has never interested me. I never read mysteries. I'm interested in what antagonists are doing and thinking and how they go about what they do. I like the world of violence. I think people who are in the criminal life are interesting. The bad guys interest me.'

The *Get Shorty* collection intrigued Travolta. But there was something wrong with the script. What was missing was Elmore Leonard's gifted dialogue. It had been paraphrased. Travolta asked for it to be put back.

Despite all the agreement and a $5 million offer plus another million for his *Pulp Fiction* Oscar nomination he still was not certain. The dragons of indecision were roaring around his head. Everybody was yelling: For Chrissakes, John!!! The polite people around Hollywood were calling him an 'asshole.' Tarantino just called him. And told him to make the movie. Travolta recalled, 'He said, "Look, man, what's going on here? This is one you say yes to." '

It was a tortured route Travolta took to give one of the finer performances of his career as minor Miami loan shark Chili Palmer who jets to Hollywood to chase schlockmeister film producer Gene Hackman for a bad gambling debt. This particular good fellow ends up with Hackman's lover Rene Russo as well as making his movies. It's a savage satire. The film with its insider jokes and lines played better in America (more than $100 million at the box office) than in Europe. Danny DeVito turns up as the ego-bound, short-stature superstar Martin Weir – the 'Shorty' of the piece – who reminded many, not unintentionally, of Dustin Hoffman who long before had been interested in that other Elmore Leonard project...

Leonard was as wary of Travolta as the actor was of taking on the role of Chili Palmer 'I was thinking De Niro, Pacino, Andy Garcia,' said Leonard. 'I saw that type playing Chili Palmer as a cool guy. Travolta had turned it down but after Quentin

Tarantino told him, "This is the one you got to do", he did it.

'I was disappointed when I first heard he had taken the role because *Pulp Fiction* hadn't been released and I remembered *Look Who's Talking*. I thought: "Oh, no, Jesus…not Travolta". But within a few weeks, and with the popularity of *Pulp Fiction*, I realised the timing couldn't have been better.'

The clock had been running a long time. In 1979 Leonard met a wiseguy called Ernest 'Chili' Palmer who had retired from the thug business and graduated to being a private detective in Miami. Leonard, the consummate listener, tapped Palmer's subconscious – his underworld – for his novels. 'He's a little rough around the edges but he's cool,' said Leonard.

In 1990 for his annual delivery of hard prose on hard men he based his best anti-hero since 'Stick' on 'Chili' Palmer. Palmer, who turns 60 in 1997, is fond of his role in the novel that skewers Hollywood self-absorption. For the movie he met and coached Travolta and explained where he got his nickname. 'Someone pegged it on me as an infant. If you said "Chili" in my neighbourhood you knew it was me. Not like Tony. We had eighty Tonys.'

What about the movie catchline? 'Look at me,' Palmer says with a stare. 'Basically it works. It's cool,' and for Rene Russo, 'John Travolta embodies cool.'

It had been Leonard's idea that when Chili Palmer wants to make his point in the film he commands, 'Look at me.' But it hadn't been a foregone conclusion that Travolta would get the role, as Elmore Leonard explained:

'The part also had to be offered to all the dinosaurs in Hollywood including Warren Beatty. Warren asked, "Why would a guy that looks like me be a loan shark? Wouldn't he be running the whole thing?" So the producer told Beatty that he had a plumber in East Hampton who was better looking.'

After years of Hollywood disappointment, the author believes they finally got it right with *Get Shorty*. And Travolta? 'He delivered his lines. He's down to earth. He called me Mr Leonard which I liked.'

That is a rave.

Which is mostly what John Woo's *Broken Arrow* received. Travolta played renegade Air Force pilot Vic Deakins, a psycho villain who hijacks two nuclear warheads ('broken arrow" is military code for a missing nuclear device), having first been offered the hero role of Riley Hale. Christian Slater played the good guy. 'I told them I only wanted to be the bad guy and after three months they said OK. Christian was eager to play more of a hero since he'd been bad in a few previous films so it all worked out. I thought the guy would have an ego and a certain amount of arrogance. He was a warmonger, yes, but different.'

Christian Slater says he found working with Travolta a different experience. 'I've worked with a lot of big stars and he's the only one who's ever actually knocked on my trailer door just to come in and talk and hang out. He even taught me the hand jive sequence from *Grease*.

'He's like some old-time movie star, like the way you'd think Cary Grant would be – smart and funny and fun to be around.'

Samantha Mathis played Slater's girl and ally in the pyrotechnical thriller – and she helped ease the tension during filming. 'We got a karaoke machine and they put on 'You're the One that I Want'. The next thing I know John drops to his knees and sings, "I got the chills, they're multiplying" and I went with it. He picked me up, he spun me around, we did the whole thing. Now I can die a happy woman: I danced with John Travolta.'

By then all of Hollywood wanted to. It changed Travolta's attitude and his look. The wary, over-cautious actor, whom everybody knew but no one really knew what to do with, was gone. And, of course, all the people who had helped keep his career coffin nailed were celebrating the most enthusiastically.

'I've never met anyone who enjoys being a movie star more than John,' says *Get Shorty* director Barry Sonnenfeld. 'It's not in terms of pushing people around or wanting a bigger camper but in terms of material wealth, showing up in a Rolls. He loves that but in a playful way. He's like a kid who's got this stuff. He embraces life, has this terrific *joie de vivre.*'

Travolta looked good on the acclaim: tanned, confident and with a bounce in his walk, the charm mannerisms searching like headlights. This was the makeover man. He had leaped out of his Tinseltown grave twenty pounds lighter, with more than $60 million – and counting – in the bank. The superstar wages – plus hefty profit percentage – turned him into the leading man of the nineties. The thin leading man.

Travolta is a gourmand.

When guests turn up for lunch it's likely to be a favourite like crab cakes, seafood lasagne with white sauce and asparagus and a salad with caramelised pecans. Dessert is often kiwi-and-strawberry-studded Napoleon. As his career all but vanished he was able to forget about his waistline and concentrate on his food.

In the *Look Who's Talking* films he was happily chubby. Serving up one-liners and bullets in *Pulp Fiction* there was plenty of weight in his menace. In *Get Shorty* he was much leaner, although gone, long gone, are the days of *Stayin' Alive* when he worked himself into a ludicrous picture of rippling muscle.

He's in shape, but fortysomething shape. His figure and his skin reflect his efforts to eat and exercise sensibly although he admits, 'It was damn hard. I like my food. I just had to be careful. There are all sorts of diets on the market – there seems to be a guru for every vegetable.

'But like everything else in life you have got to find a regimen that works for your lifestyle. And your personality. You don't want to suffer too much. I knew it was important for the films I was going to make to make the effort. Some of the characters I was going to play wouldn't have the extra pounds or chins.'

He created the Travolta diet to accommodate himself. It helps to be reasonably well-off. His hamburgers are made from ground *filet mignon*. He loves dessert – and will order three at a time. The trick is that he only has a small taste of each. He hardly uses alcohol and his tipple is iced tea. Or rather, it is his passion. He just doesn't want passion flowers in it.

In America, and California in particular, they insist on serving iced tea in an endless combination of flavours. It irks Travolta. 'The only evil urge I admit is to shoot people responsible for flavouring iced tea.'

These days he eats grilled fish, usually sole, with salad and asparagus washed down by 'real' iced tea. As with everything else he insists on his tea being the way he wants it. He's not horrid about this but will wait until finally – sometimes at the fourth attempt – a waiter will deliver the real thing.

It brings a smile. As does his wife.

But especially 33-year-old Mrs Travolta. During the filming of *Get Shorty* the couple would sneak off to one of California's 'no tell' motels to spend intimate time together. One of the film's assistants said, 'He's lost a great deal of weight and maintains the reason why he looks so good is because of his and Kelly's favourite form of exercise. He told me, "Some people like yoga, some like swimming or running. But there's nothing as pleasurable, healthful and rewarding as a good round of vigorous lovemaking." John could have gone off to some ritzy hotel suite but he liked the fun of going to those motels.'

Suddenly, working was also fun again. In *Premiere* magazine's list of Hollywood's 100 Most Powerful People published in the summer of 1996 he was ranked number 47. From nowhere the previous year. In the magazine's British edition published at the same time he was number 16 in a list of the year's 25 most powerful actors leaving Sharon Stone, Robert De Niro and Demi Moore in his wake.

In the American list Quentin Tarantino appeared at number 71. Barbra Streisand was at 85, Martin Scorsese at 58. Jack Nicholson scraped in at number 91.

Prior to this, though, Universal Studios had rejected Nora Ephron's movie *Michael*, about an oversexed angel, when she insisted on casting Travolta rather than Nicholson as her angel. Her 'risk' casting is paying off with her film soaring as it is along Travolta's rainbow.

Travolta felt content with his own family around and it helped him deal with the loss of his father who was 84 when his bad heart finally failed him on 29 May 1995. He also had a fright when his wife was in a car accident near their home at Maine's Penobscot Bay. Kelly was driving through a blizzard to get two of their staff to a ferry boat when her Jeep crashed into a telegraph pole. She and the two passengers were not hurt.

Perils surfaced directly involved with his reincarnated stardom. The couple were sued by lawyer Bob Cohen who had rented them his Beverly Hills home in 1994/1995. He said the Travoltas were in breach of contract and had caused $500,000 worth of damage to the home. Travolta's lawyer Martin Singer countered, 'They left the place in immaculate shape.'

These were annoyances. Travolta was pleased and proud that his father had lived to see his youngest son's son. The family lessons had stayed learned; the Travoltas remained and remain close.

He says there is never a night when his mother or someone else close like Diana Hyland is not in his dreams. Sometimes he resents waking up for the ghosts of the past have gone. Travolta, against the betting by the best, the specialists, the experts, the bullshitters, and all conventional wisdom, is still around. Alive and kicking too.

In July 1996, *Phenomenon* lived up to its name with its position at number two in the US box-office charts, second only to the highest-grossing film of all time, *Independence Day*.

They staged an elaborate wrap party when *Phenomenon* finished filming. There was lots of singing and dancing and Travolta had plenty of partners.

'There's this thing: people feel it would be fun for them to dance with me. And of course they'll play some song from *Saturday Night Fever* that I have to deal with. Then I kind of – not cringe, but think, "OK, once this song is over I'll be able to have some fun."

'My fear is that they'll clear this floor and I'll have to perform solo. And that I don't want to do. At 200lbs weight doing those knee dips is a little tough…'

Forget the knees. There's a lot of weight on John Travolta's shoulders to keep delivering.

And, as Chuck Berry sings, 'You Never Can Tell.'

FEVER!

The filmography of
JOHN TRAVOLTA

* Including US domestic box office gross

1975

The Devil's Rain Rank.
Director: Robert Fuest. Starring Ernest Borgnine.
Ida Lupino, William Shatner, John Travolta.

Travolta's big screen debut in a movie about Satanic worshippers seeking the names of a list of souls promised to the Devil. He melts in a puddle of liquid putrescence shouting 'Blasphemer! Blasphemer!' **$17 million.**

1976

The Boy in the Plastic Bubble Made-for-television movie.
Director: Randal Kleiser.
Starring John Travolta, Diana Hyland.

A television film about a boy born with immune deficiencies that force him to live in a protective bubble.
* Not applicable.

1976

Carrie United Artists.
Director: Brian De Palma. Starring: Sissy Spacek, Amy Irving, Piper Laurie, William Katt and John Travolta.

Carrie's supposed prom date Travolta is tough guy Billy seduced by a scheming cheerleader in the first screen adaptation of a Stephen King novel. ***$34 million**

1977

Saturday Night Fever Paramount Pictures.
Director: John Badham.
Starring John Travolta, Karen Lynn Gorney.

Travolta earned his first Oscar nomination for his classic portrayal of disco king Tony Manero.
* $94 million (International: $142 million).

1978

Grease Paramount Pictures.
Director: Randal Kleiser. Starring **John Travolta, Olivia Newton-John, Stockard Channing, Jeff Conaway, Sid Caesar, Joan Blondell, Frankie Avalon.**

Travolta sings, dances and goofs as Danny Zuko to Newton-John's Sandy in the adaptation based on the Broadway show. ***$153 million. (International: $186 million).**

1978

Moment by Moment Universal Pictures.
Director: **Jane Wagner.**
Starring **John Travolta, Lily Tomlin.**

Sex object role reversal film with Travolta as the toy boy. ***$4.6 million.**

1980

Urban Cowboy Paramount Pictures.
Director: **James Bridges.** Starring **John Travolta, Debra Winger, Scott Glenn, Madolyn Smith.**

Travolta's Bud is a young stud who finds the love of strong woman Debra Winger. *** $47 million.**

1981

Blow Out Filmways Pictures.
Director: **Brian De Palma.** Starring **John Travolta, Dennis Franz, John Lithgow, Nancy Allen.**

Travolta plays a sound effects technician in a remake of Michelangelo Antonioni's 1967 Vanessa Redgrave/David Hemmings classic 'Blow Up.' *** $16 million.**

1983

Staying Alive Paramount Pictures.
Director: **Sylvester Stallone.** Starring **John Travolta, Finola Hughes, Cynthia Rhodes.**

Travolta's Tony Manero trades in disco for Broadway. *** $64 million.**

1983

Two of a Kind Twentieth Century Fox.
Director **John Herzfeld.** Starring **John Travolta, Olivia Newton-John, Oliver Reed, Beatrice Straight, Charles Durning, Scatman Crothers.**

Angelic comedy reunites 'Grease' stars. *** $24 million.**

1985

Perfect Columbia Pictures.
Director: **James Bridges.** Starring **John Travolta, Jamie Lee Curtis, Marilu Henner.**

Travolta as 'Rolling Stone' style reporter investigating health clubs and the incredibly-exercised Jamie Lee Curtis body. Reunited him with 'Urban Cowboy' director. *** $13 million.**

1989

The Experts Paramount Pictures.
Director: **David Thomas.**
Starring **John Travolta, Kelly Preston.**

Travolta and his future wife in a comedy about Russian spies. ***$169,203.**

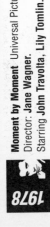

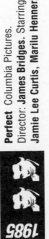

1989

Look Who's Talking TriStar Pictures.
Director: **Amy Heckerling.** Starring **John Travolta, Kirstie Alley, Bruce Willis, Abe Vigoda, George Segal, Olympia Dukakis.**

Taxi driver Travolta in 'talking' baby comedy.
* **$ 140 million.** *(International gross: $149 million).*

1990

Look Who's Talking Too TriStar Pictures.
Director: **Amy Heckerling.** Starring **John Travolta, Kirstie Alley and voices supplied by Bruce Willis, Mel Brooks and Roseanne Barr.**

A baby sister is added to the family plot.
* **$48 million**
(International gross $68 million).

1991

Shout Universal Pictures.
Director: **Jeffrey Hornaday.**
Starring **John Travolta, Linda Fiorentino.**

Travolta as a band master tries to reform 1950s delinquents with rock 'n roll.
* **$3.4 million.**

1992

Boris and Natasha: The Movie MCEG.
Director: **Charlie Martin Smith.**
Starring **John Travolta.**

Live-action version of cartoon characters.
* **No theatrical release.**

1992

Chains of Gold MCEG
Director: **Rod Holcomb.** Starring **John Travolta, Bernie Casey, Marilu Henner.**

Social worker Travolta tires to rescue boy caught in street gang drug ring.
* **No theatrical release.**

1993

Look Who's Talking Now TriStar Pictures.
Director: **Tom Ropelewski.**
Starring **John Travolta, Kirstie Alley.**

Dogs bring havoc to the lives of the Umbriacco family in the final film of the trilogy.
* **$10 million.**

1994

Eyes of An Angel (The Tender) independent.
Director: **Robert Harmon.**
Starring **John Travolta.**

Travolta flees with his daughter from mobsters; her dog follows them across America.
* **No theatrical release.**

1994

Pulp Fiction Miramax.
Director: **Quentin Tarantino.** Starring **John Travolta, Uma Thurman, Bruce Willis, Samuel L.Jackson, Tim Roth, Amanda Plummer, Eric Stoltz, Harvey Keitel, Quentin Tarantino, Rosanna Arquette, Christopher Walken.**

Travolta as heroin-addicted hit man Vincent Vega was what audiences and Hollywood had been waiting for.
* **$108 million (International gross $103 million).**

1995

Get Shorty MGM. Director: **Barry Sonnenfeld**. Starring **John Travolta, Gene Hackman, Renne Russo, Danny DeVito.**

Travolta as ultracool loan shark Chilli Palmer who wants to be a Hollywood producer.
* $89 million (to April, 1996).

1995

White Man's Burden Savoy Pictures. Director: **Desmond Nakano.** Starring **John Travolta, Harry Belafonte.**

Travolta finds himself in reverse racial prejudice drama.
* $2 million.

1996

Broken Arrow Twentieth Century Fox. Director: **John Woo**. Starring **John Travolta, Christian Slater, Samantha Mathis.**

Travolta's the turncoat airman villain, the psycho pilot, in nuclear blackmail shoot 'em up.
* $45 million (to April, 1996)

1996

Phenomenon Touchstone Pictures. Director: **Jon Turteltaub**. Starring **John Travolta, Kyra Sedgwick, Robert Duvall, Forest Whitaker.**

Travolta is the 'ordinary Joe' who finds his IQ soars overnight.
* $50 million (to July, 1996)

1996

Michael Turner Pictures. Director: **Nora Ephron**. Starring **John Travolta, William Hurt, Andie MacDowell.**

Travolta is the title character angel with 'dirty' wings – and habits in the fantasy comedy.
* N/A

1997

Dark Horse Twentieth Century Fox. Director: **Ron Howard.** Starring **John Travolta.**

Travolta at the centre of bad boy Texas politics set for 1997 release.
* N/A

1997

Face Off Paramount. Director: to be set. Starring **John Travolta and Nicolas Cage.**

Travolta and Cage in a terrorist stand-off.
* N/A

FEVER!
The index